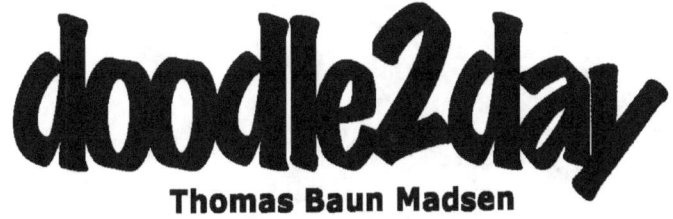

Thomas Baun Madsen

Intro

Hello, my name is Thomas, the creator of this coloring book.

I would like to thank you for taking an interest
in the doodles I have made.

Thank you!

In this coloring book you will find 40 abstract drawings
that are meant to inspire you. The designs are
a mix of mandalas and full frame patterns.

You might discover eyes, faces, flowers, animals
or something entirely different in the many intricate shapes.
Color how you like, relax and let your creativity flow.
Great when you need to unwind and recharge.

I recommend using a piece of paper between pages to stop color bleed through.

I hope you have a great time coloring!

If you want to explore more of my doodle art please visit

www.doodle2day.com

This book belongs to

_____

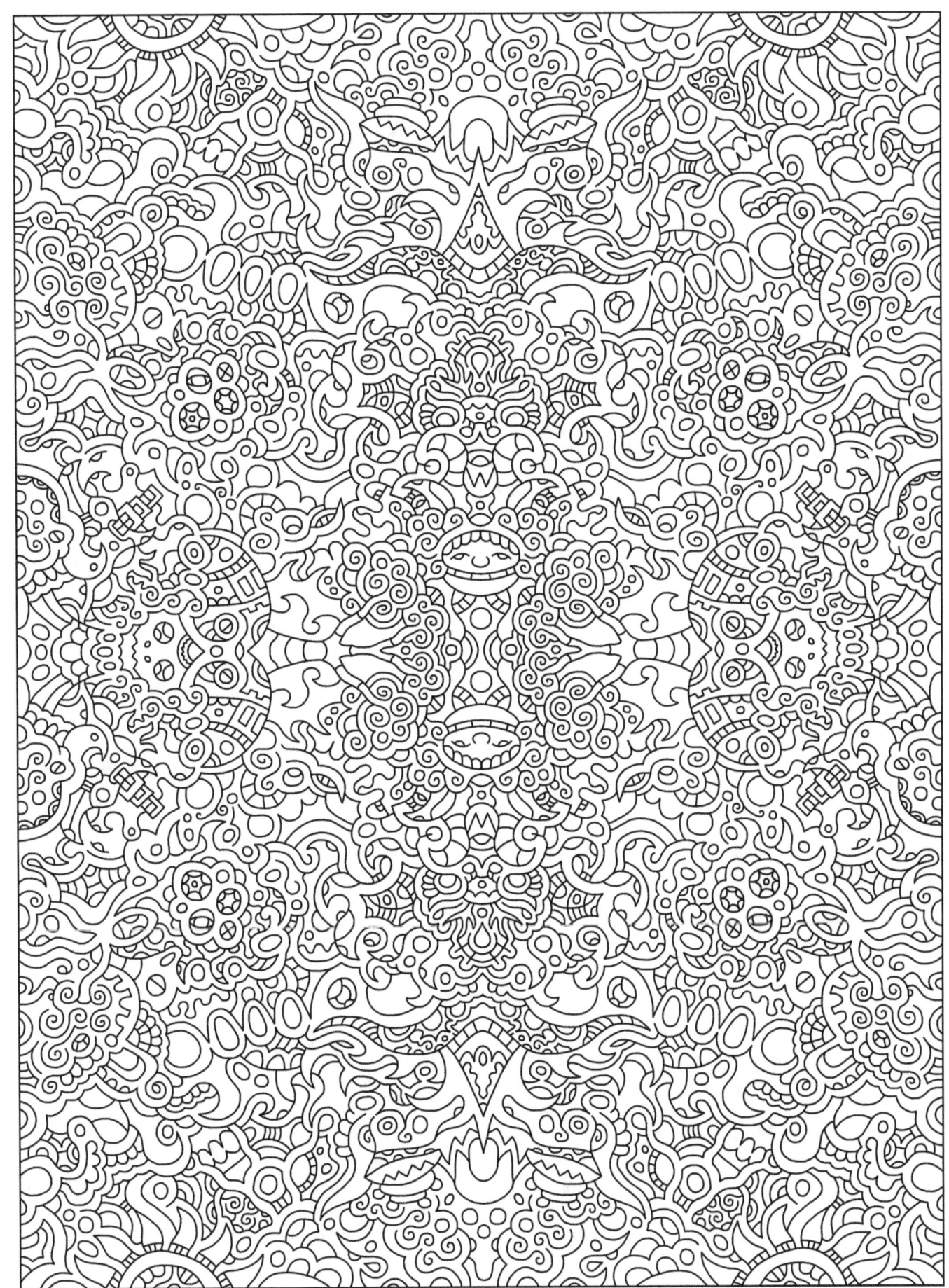

Drawing # 1

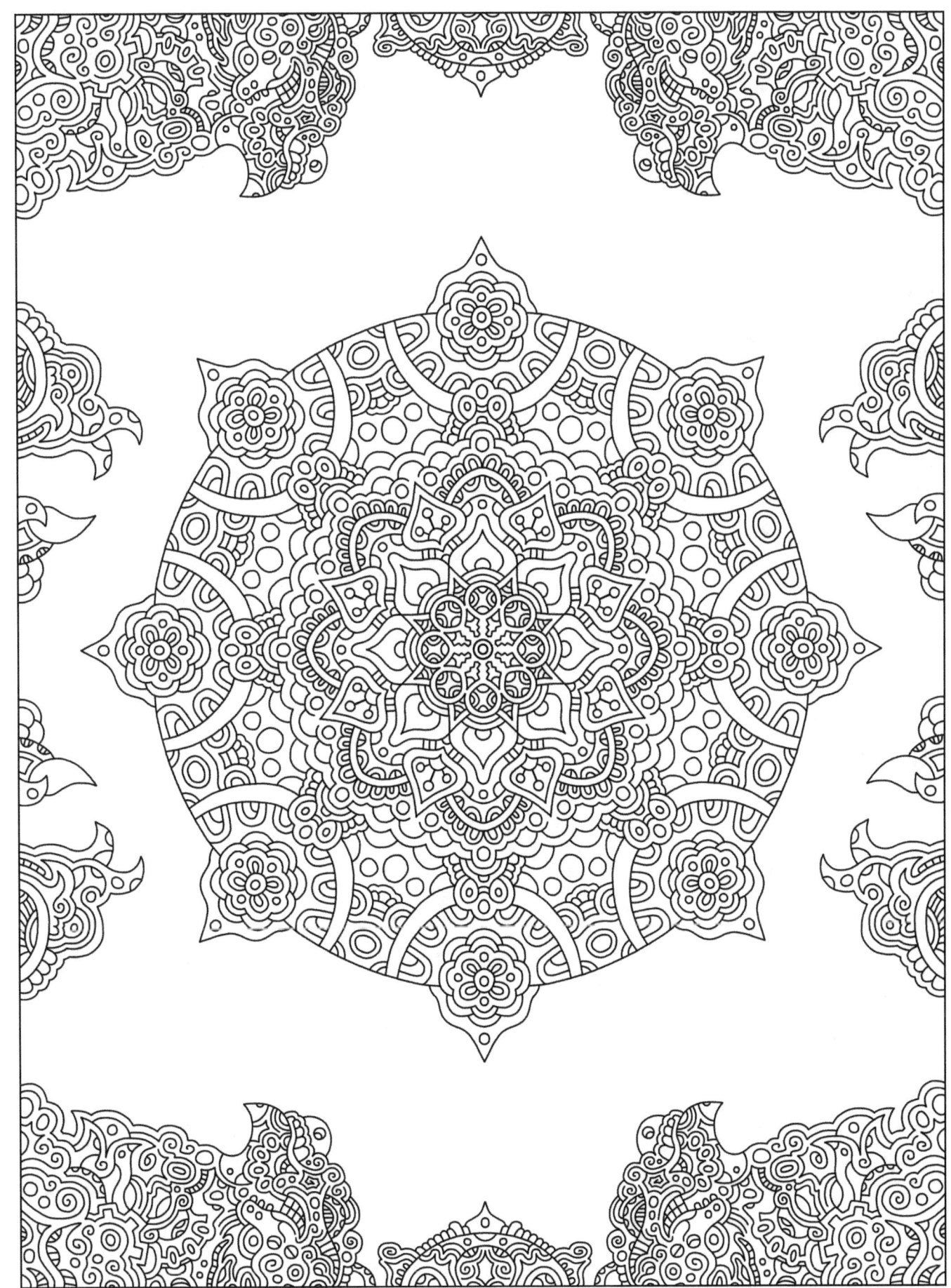

Drawing # 2

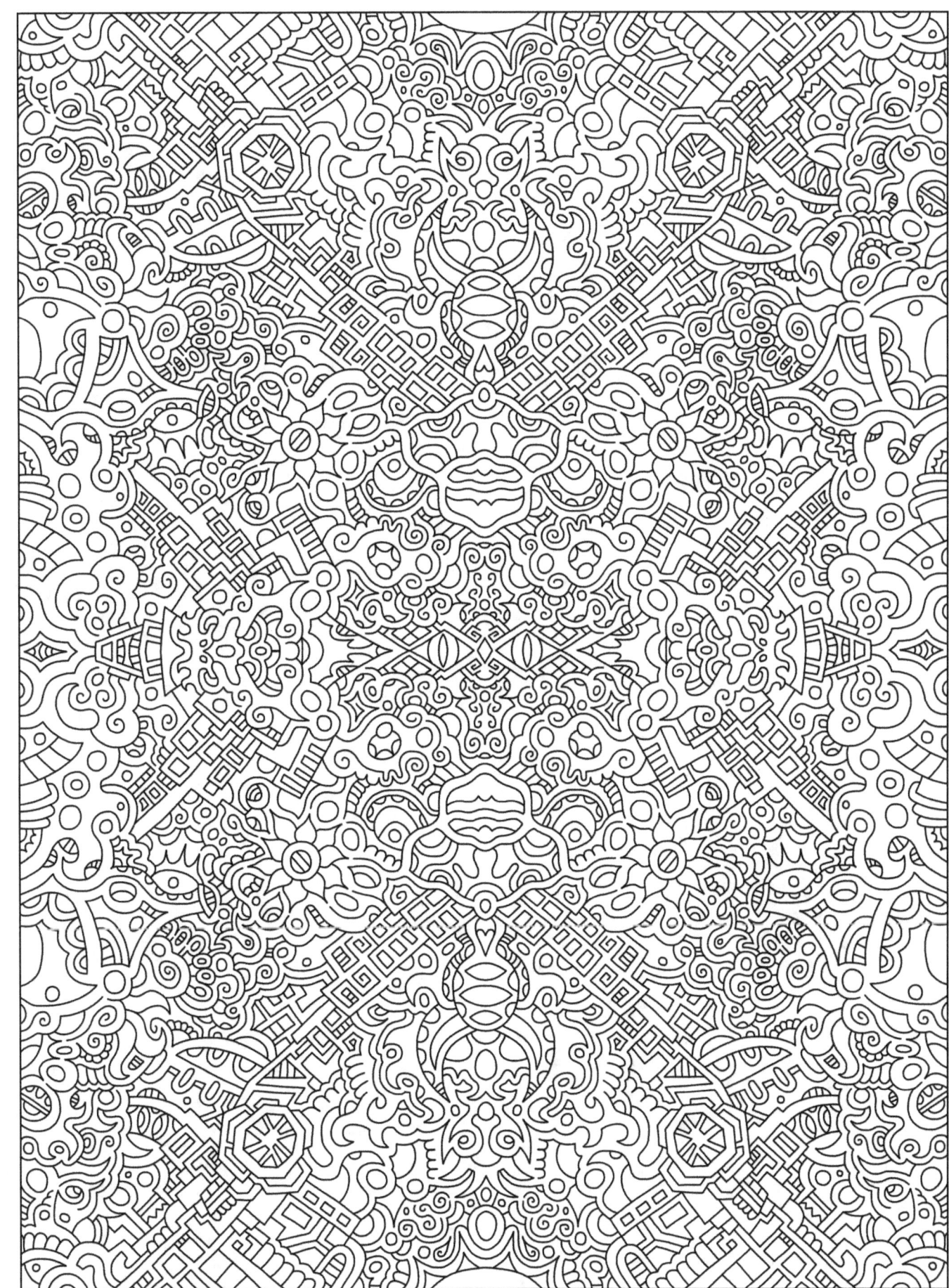

Drawing # 3

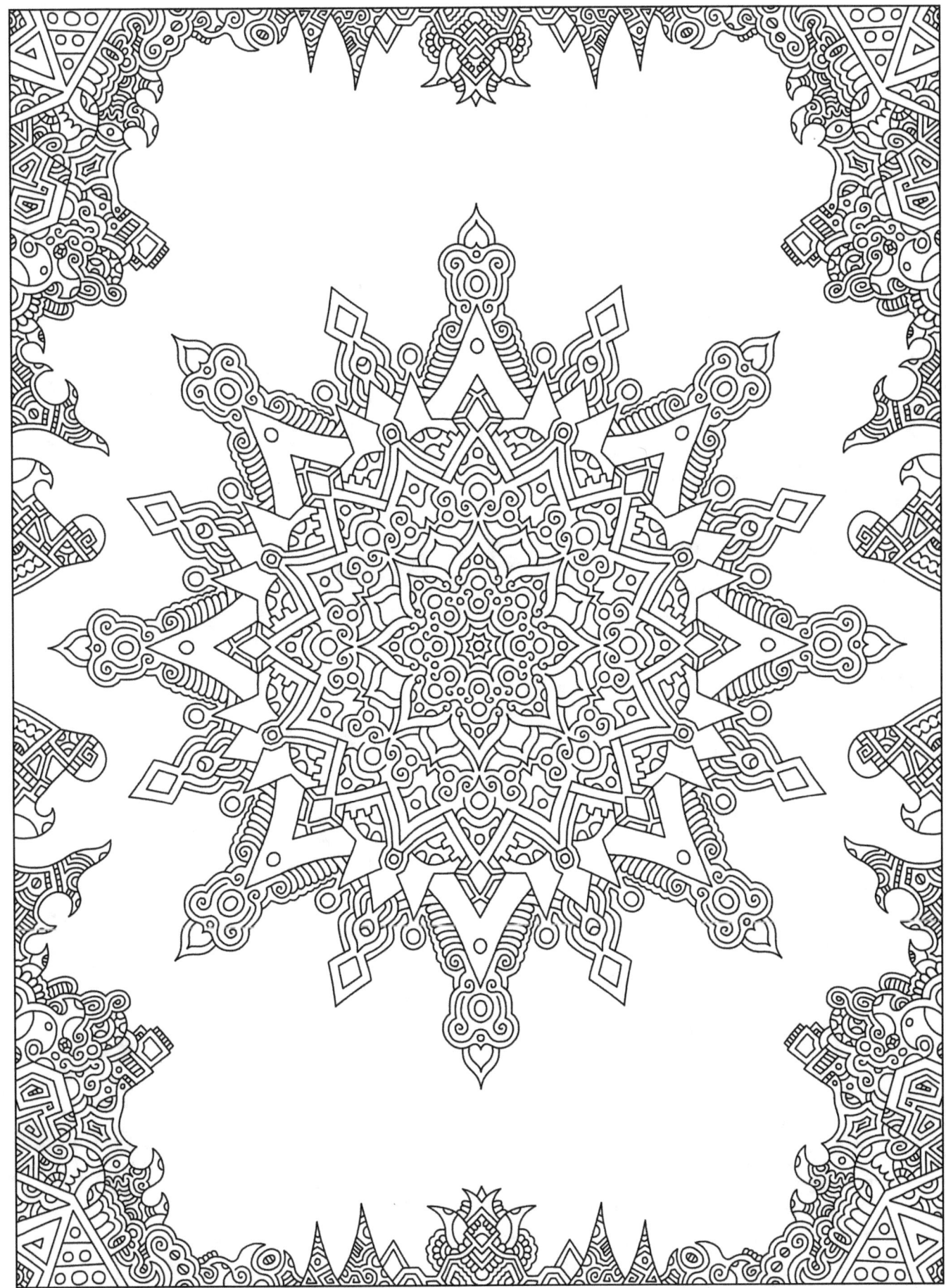

Drawing # 4

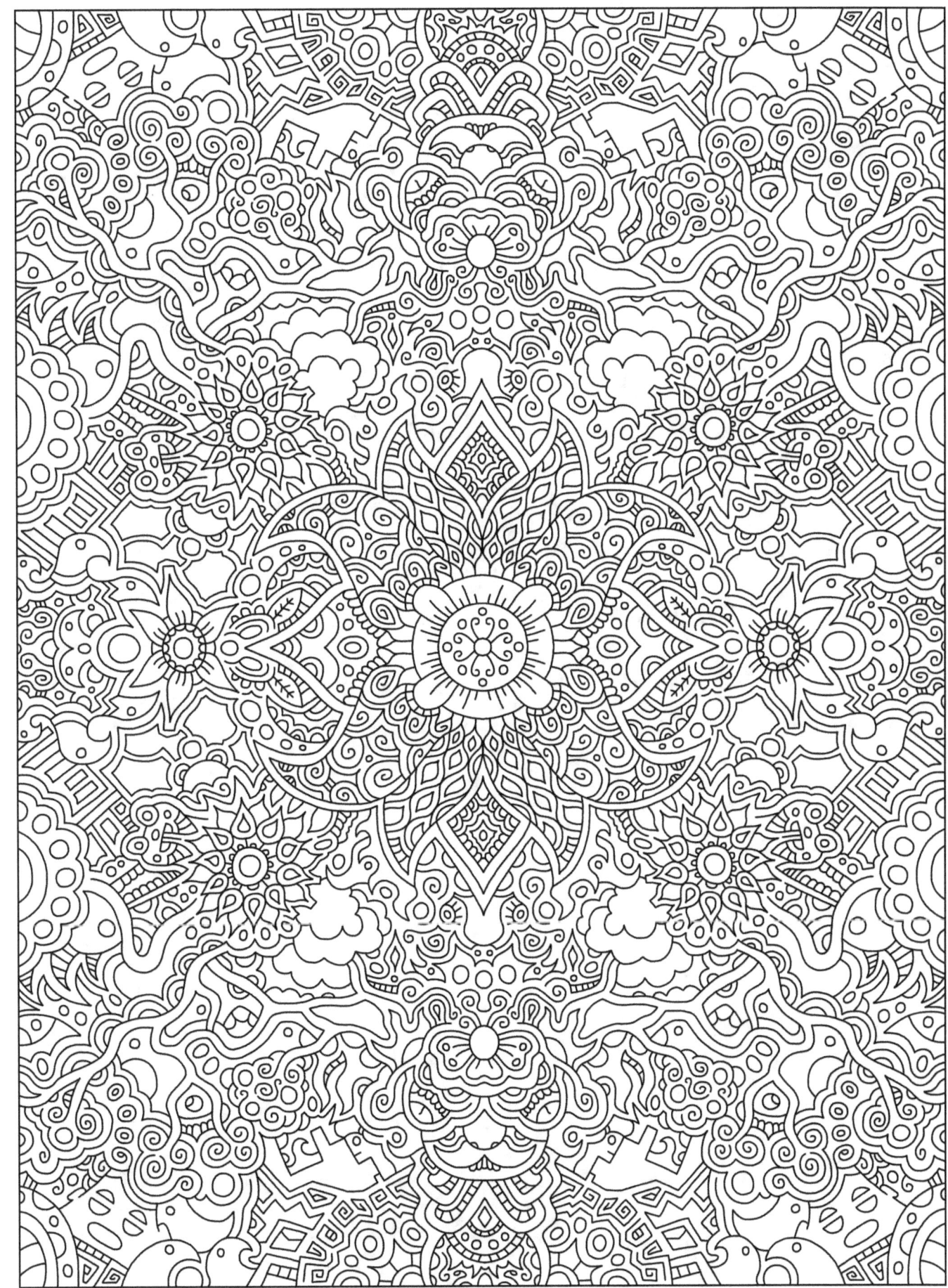

Drawing # 5

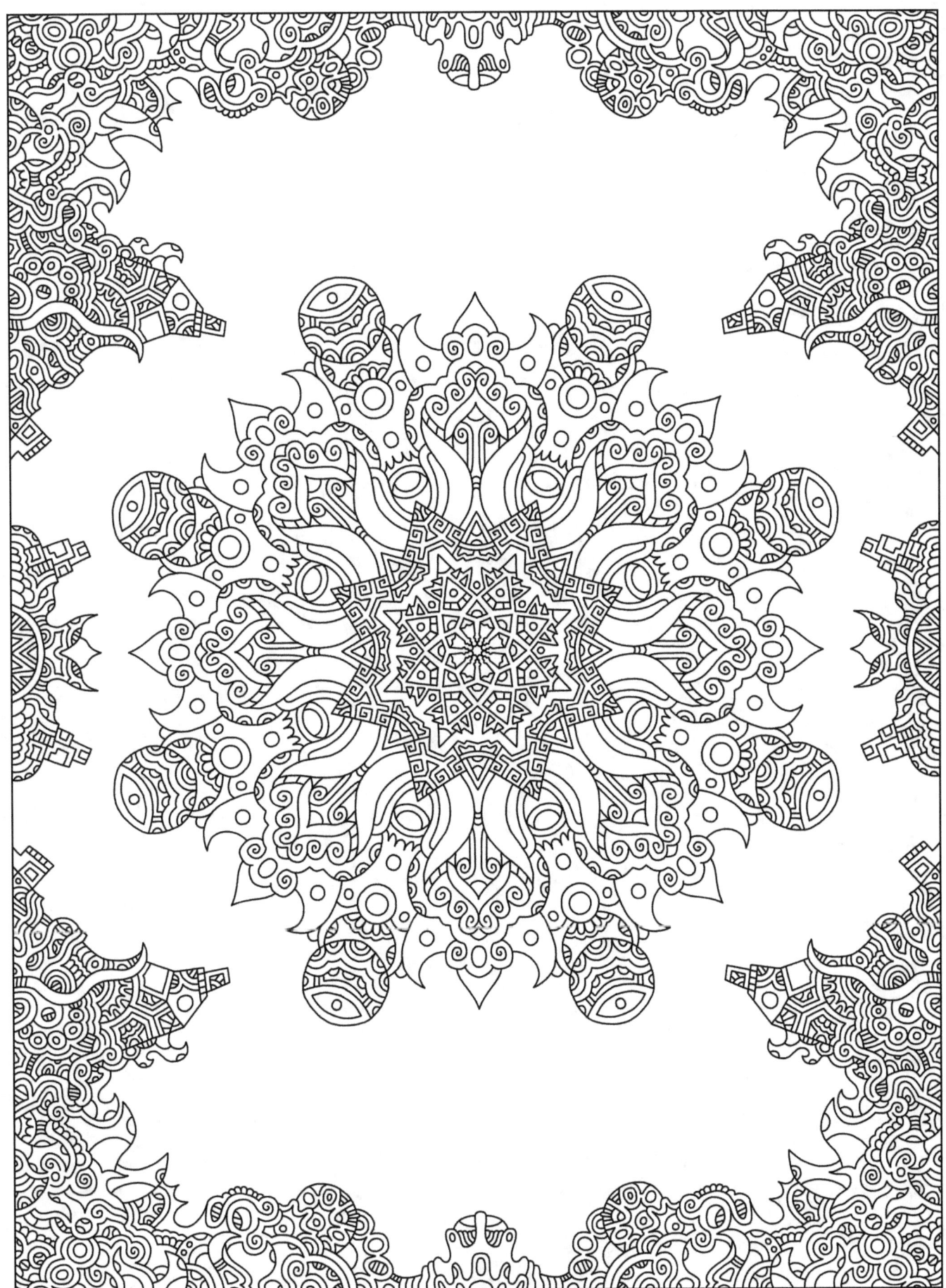

Drawing # 6

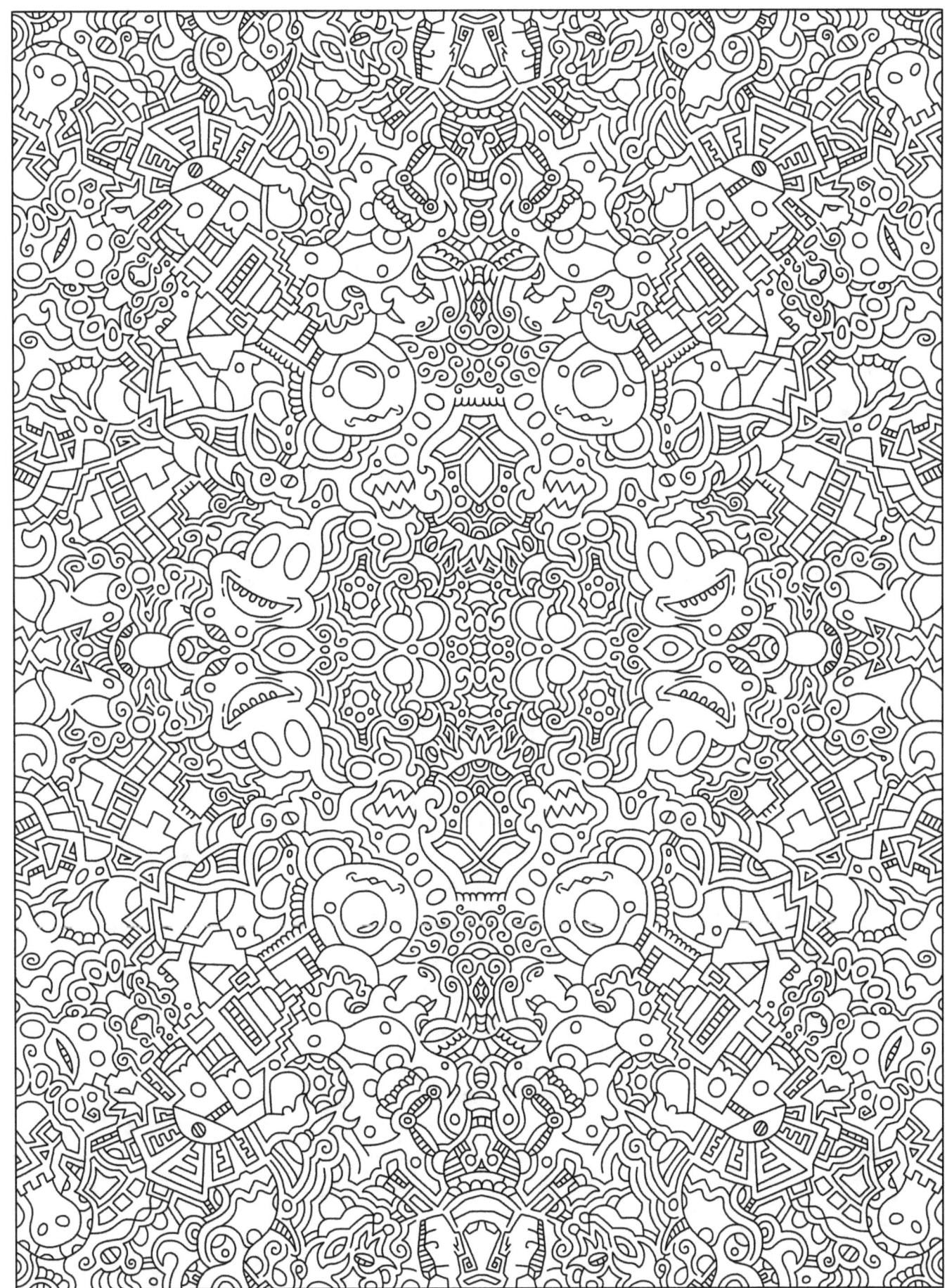

Drawing # 7

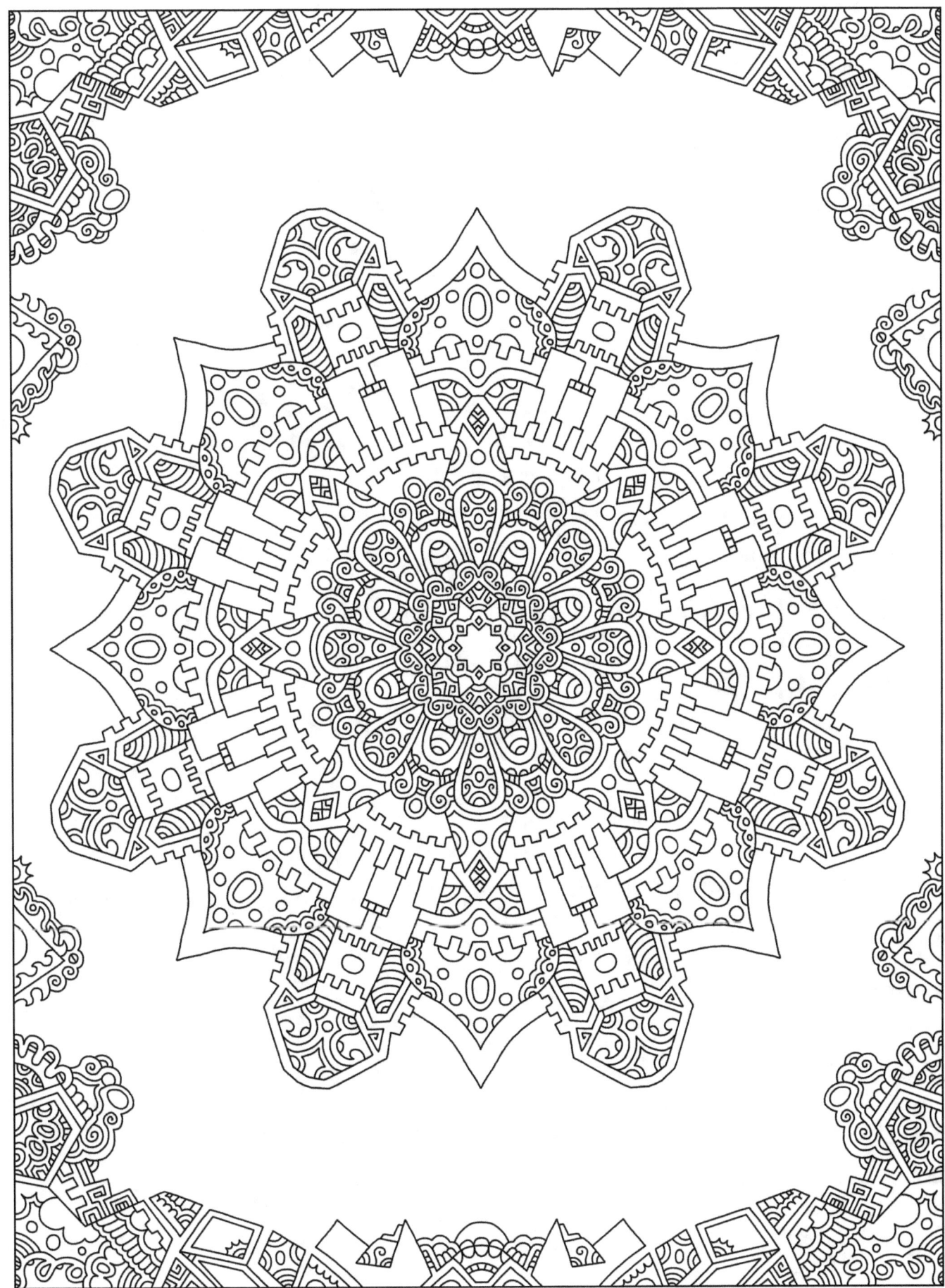

Drawing # 8

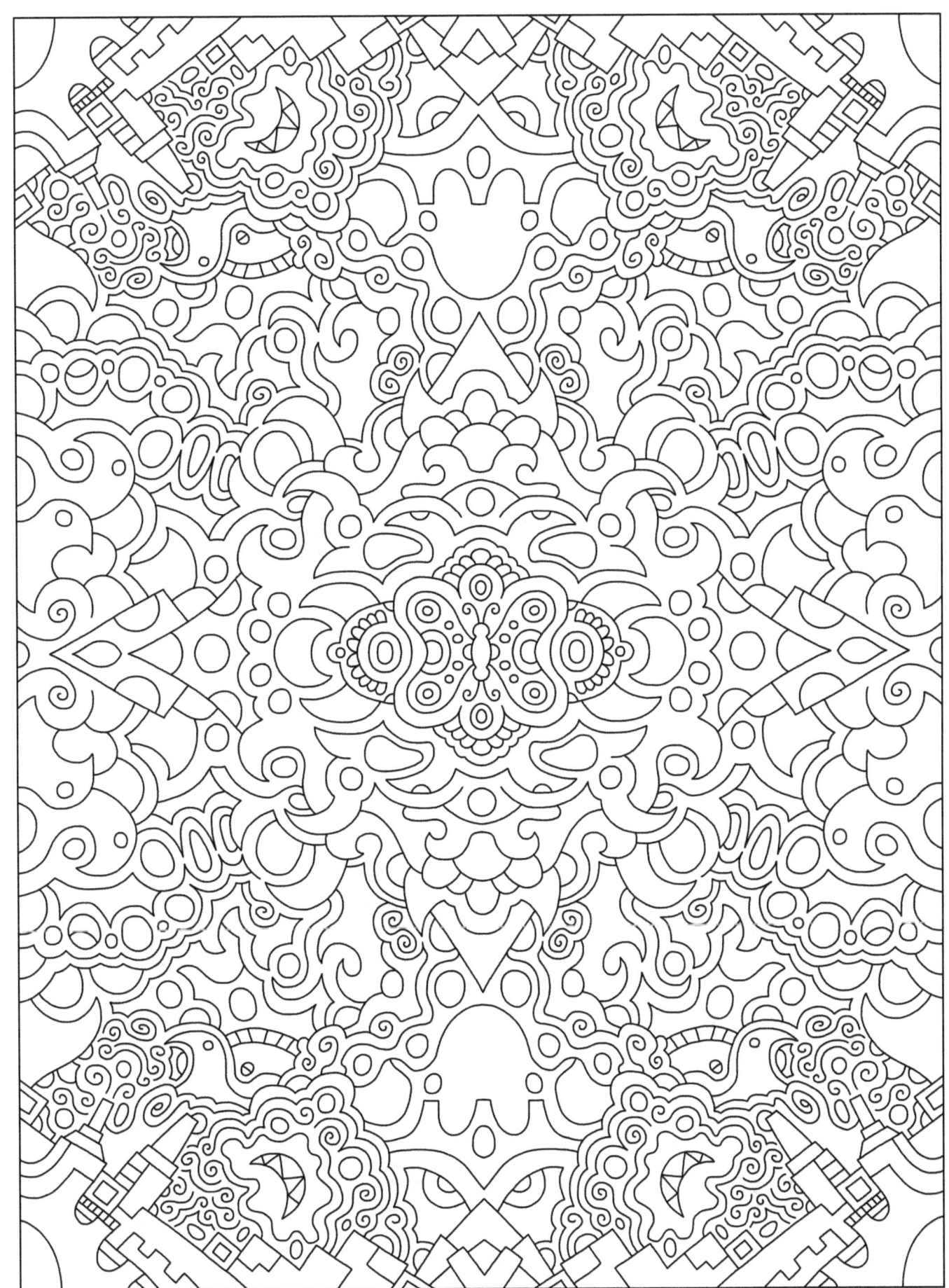

Drawing # 9

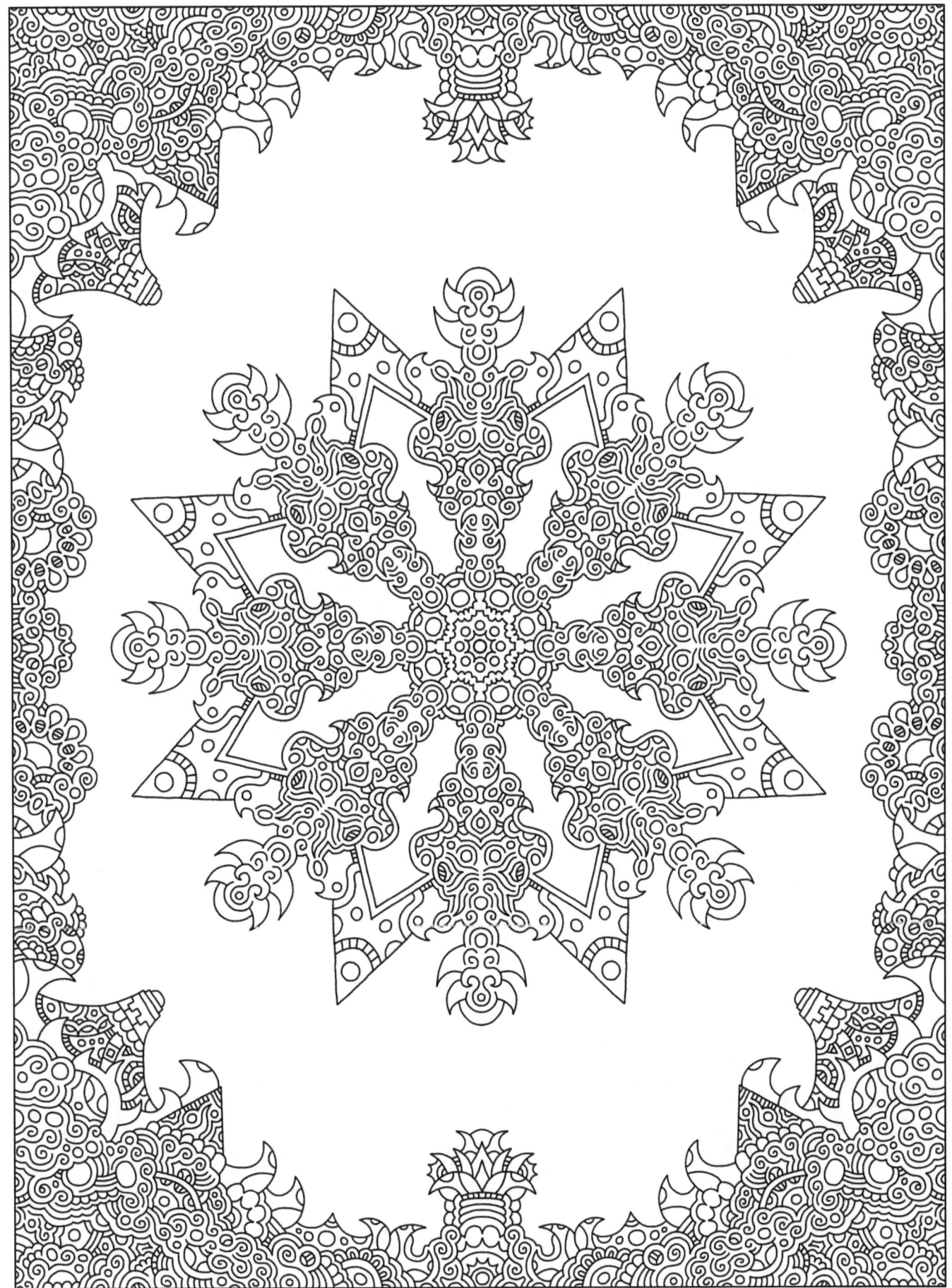

Drawing #10

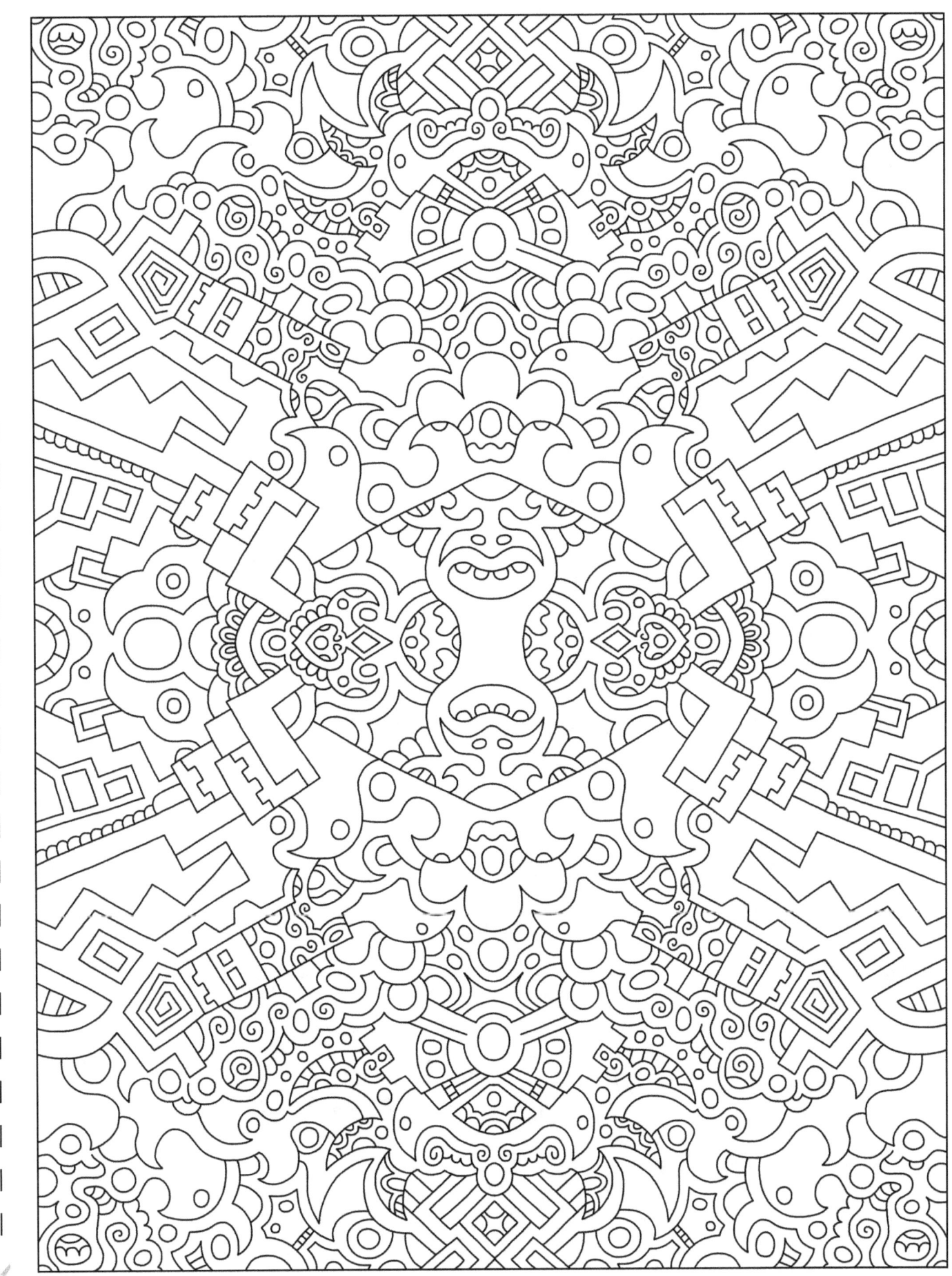

Drawing #11

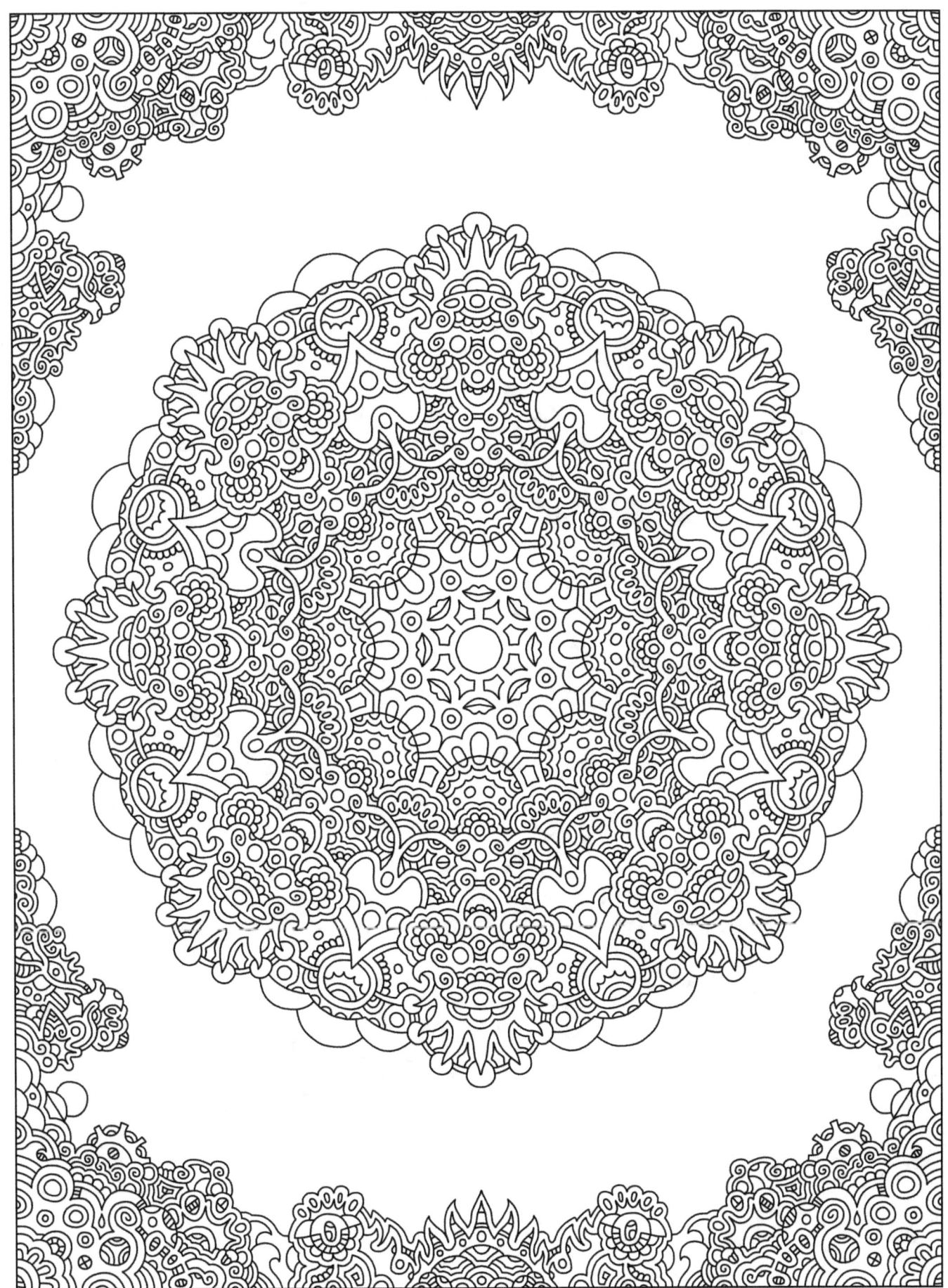

Drawing #12

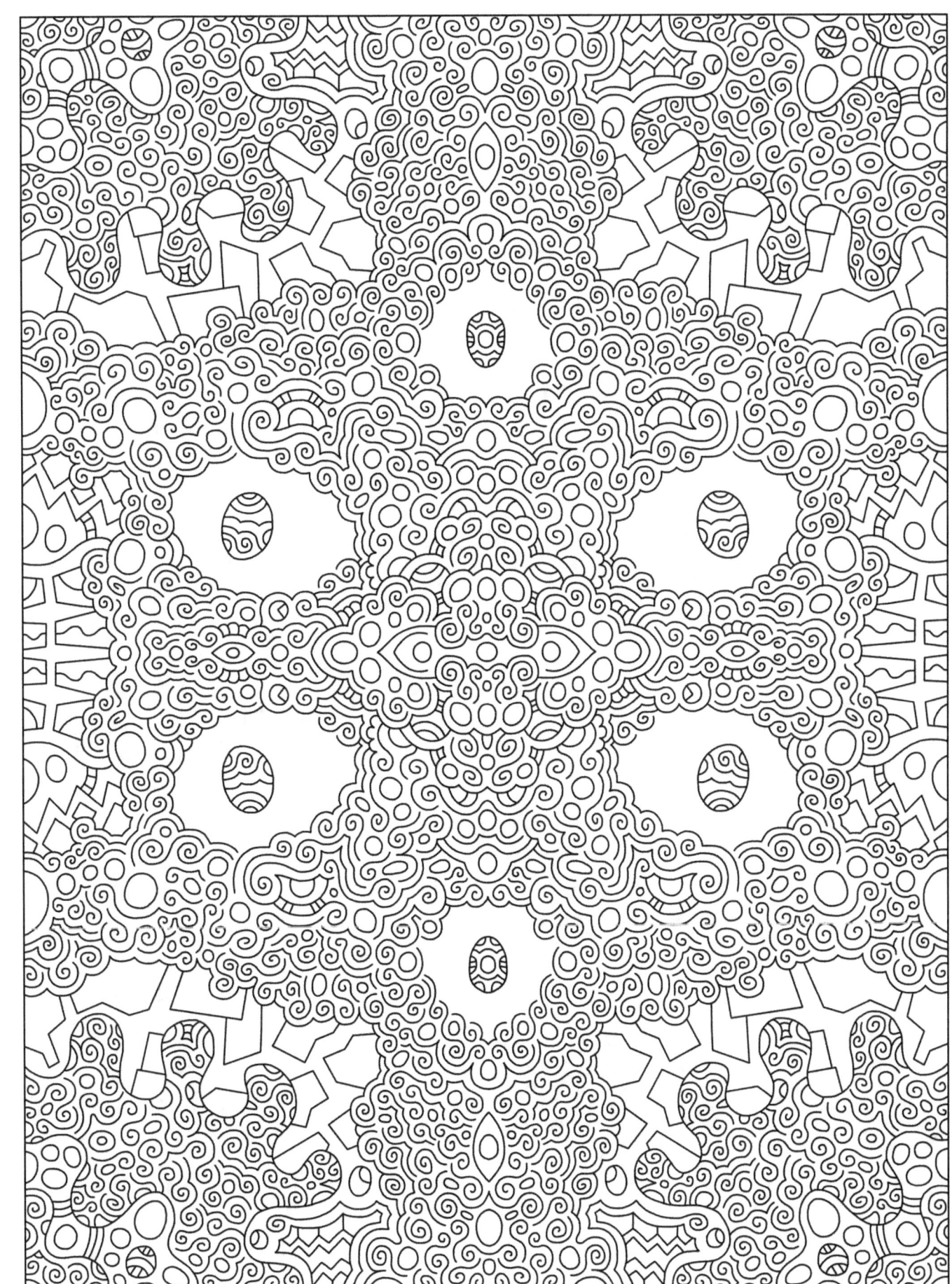

Drawing #13

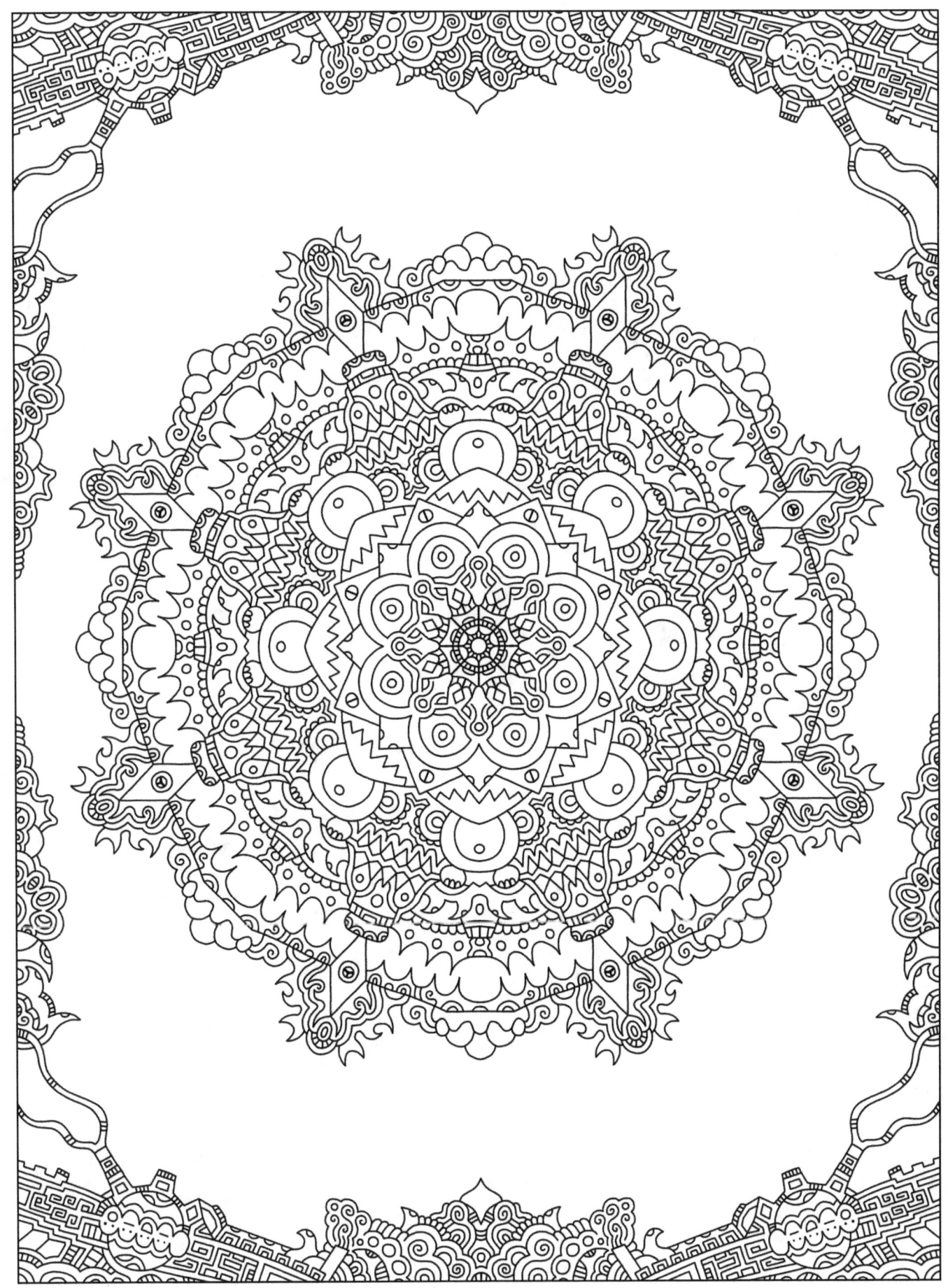

Drawing #14

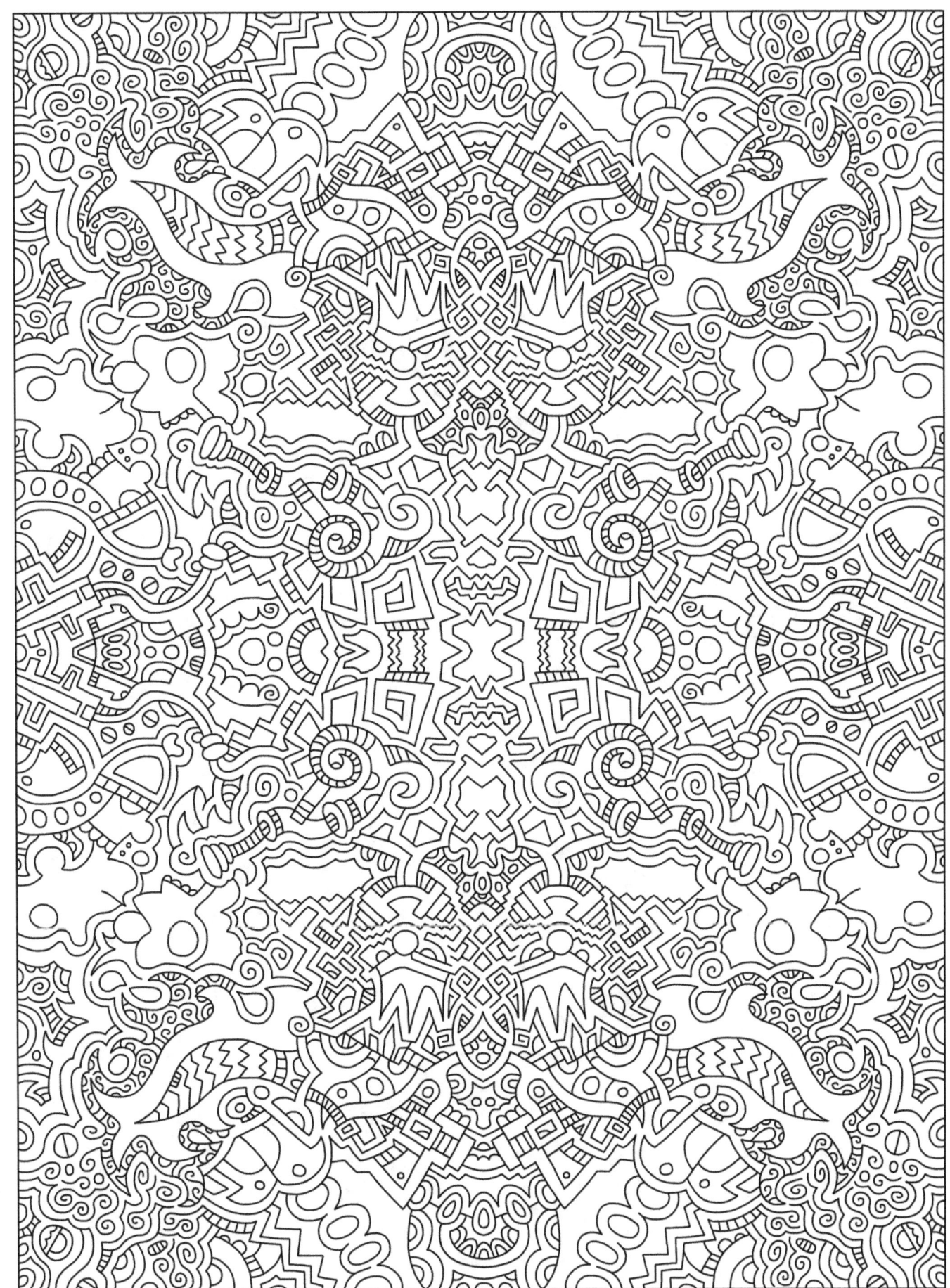

Drawing #15

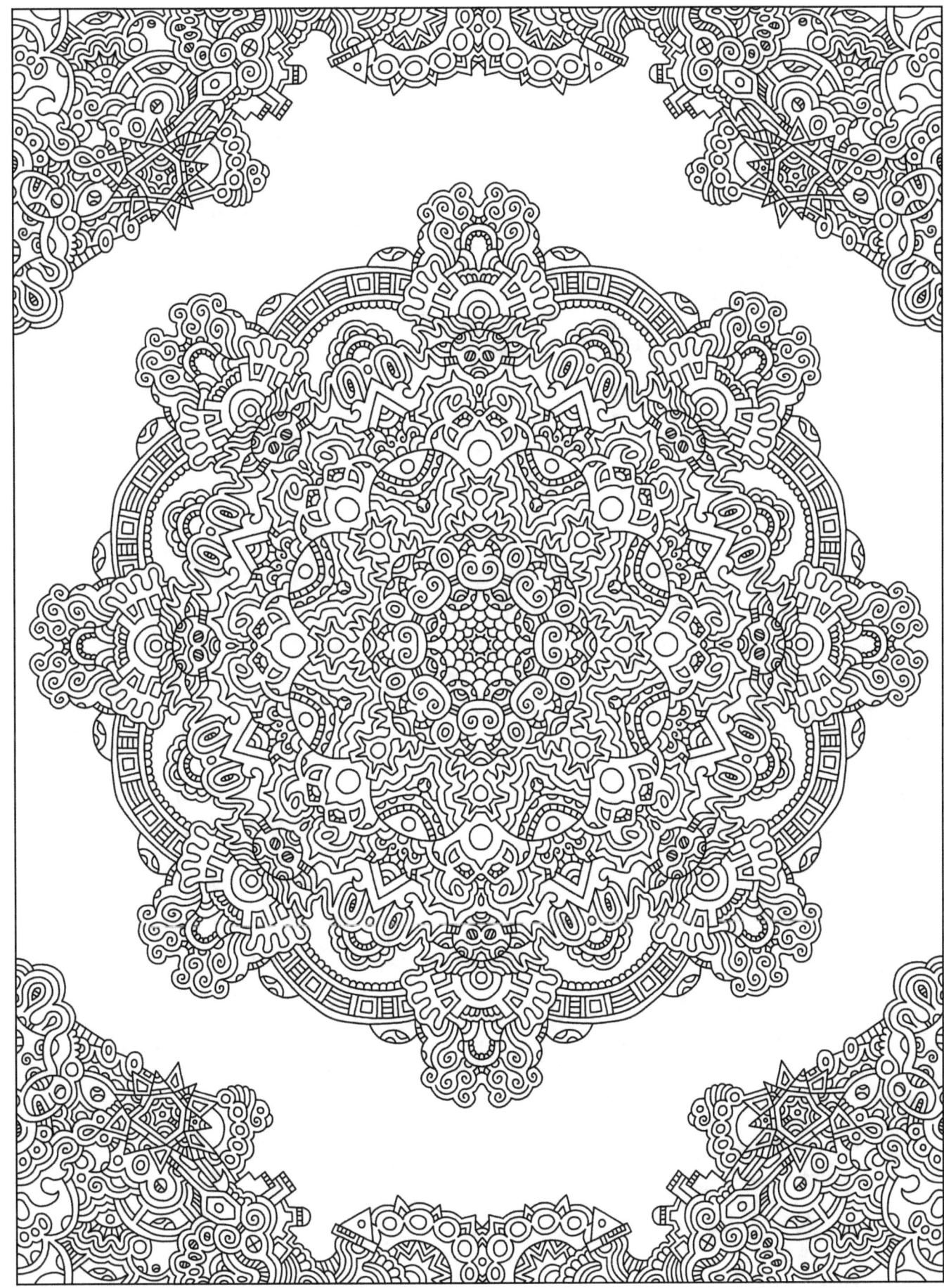

Drawing #16

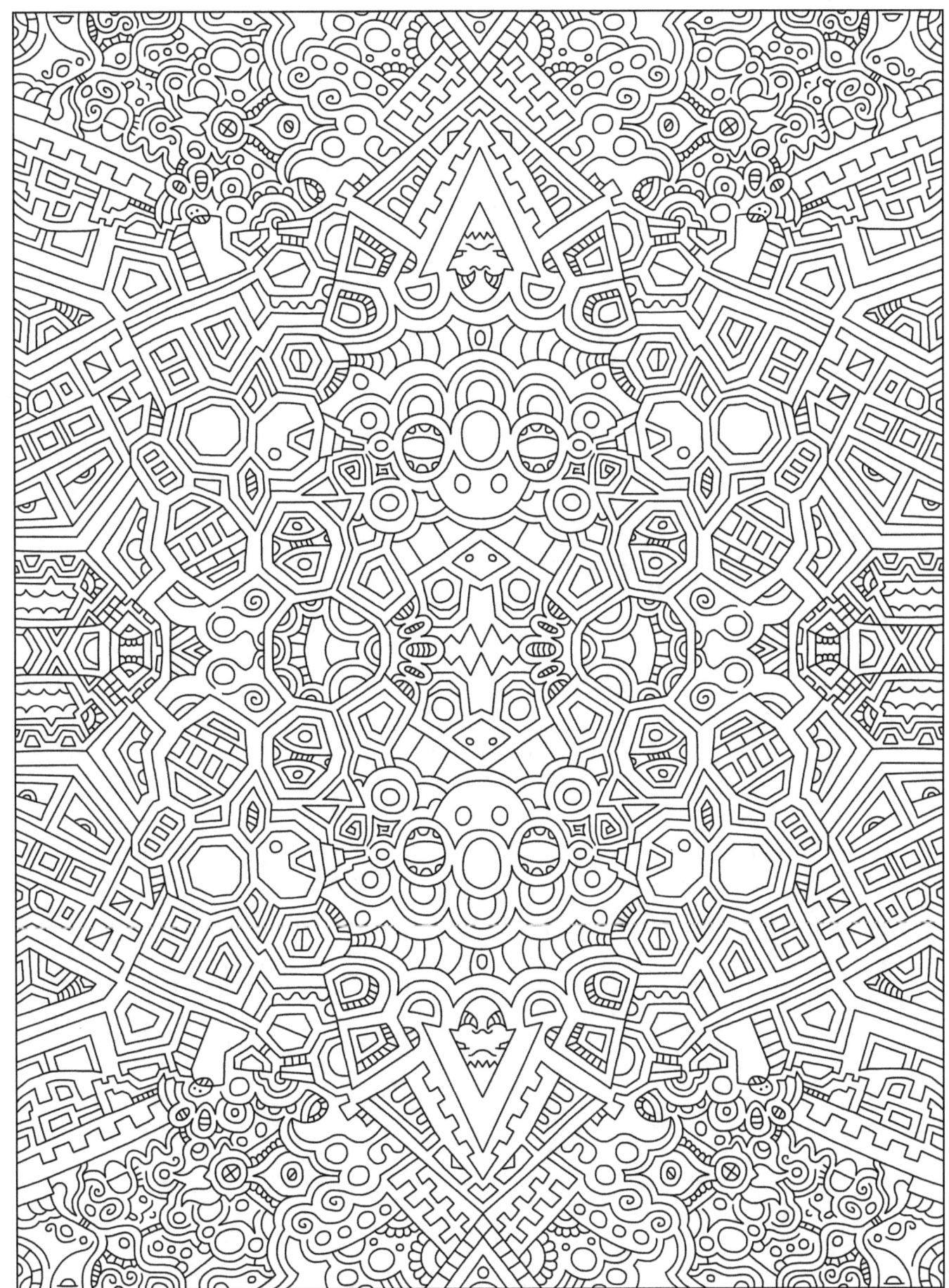

Drawing #17

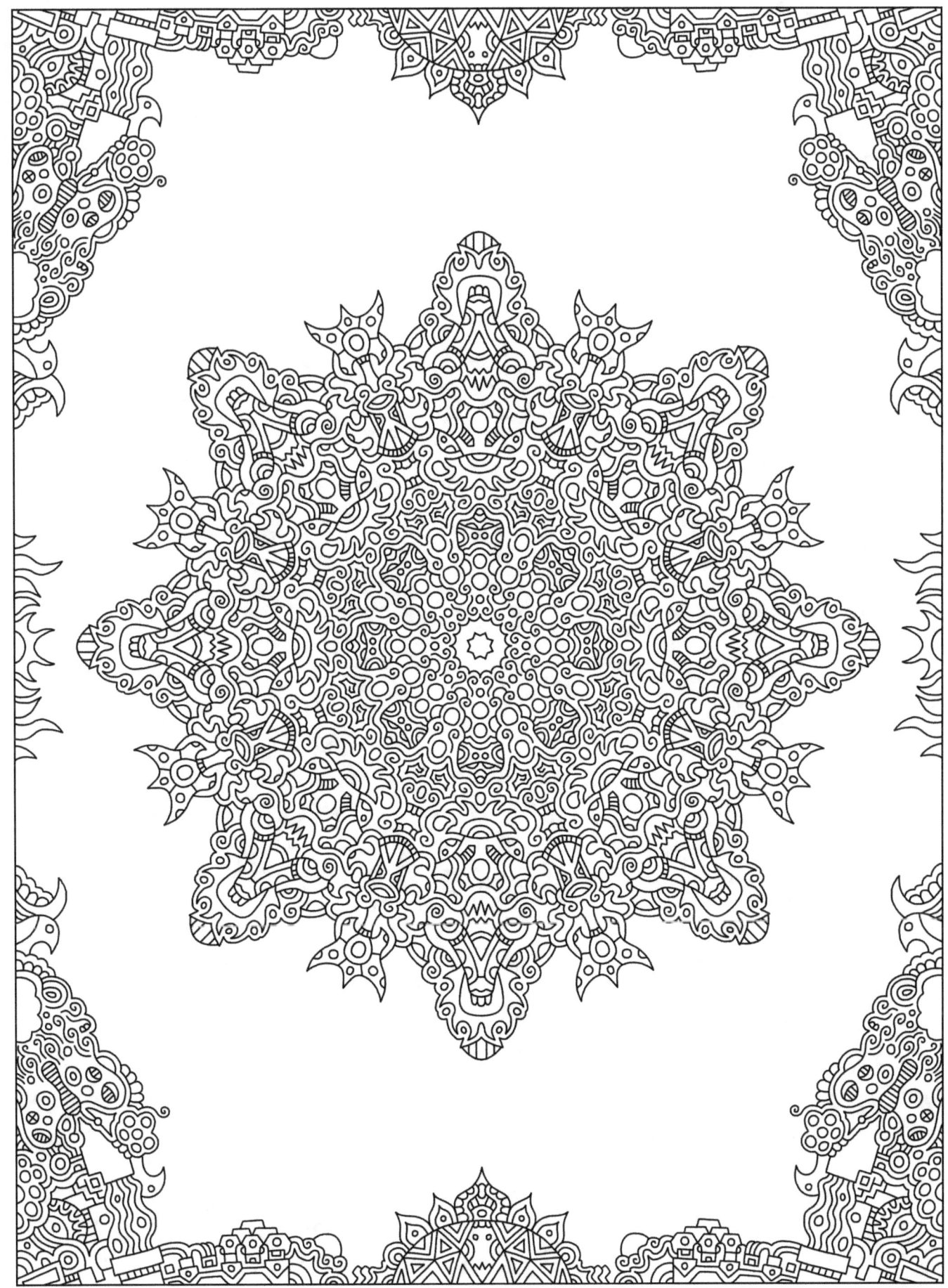

Drawing #18

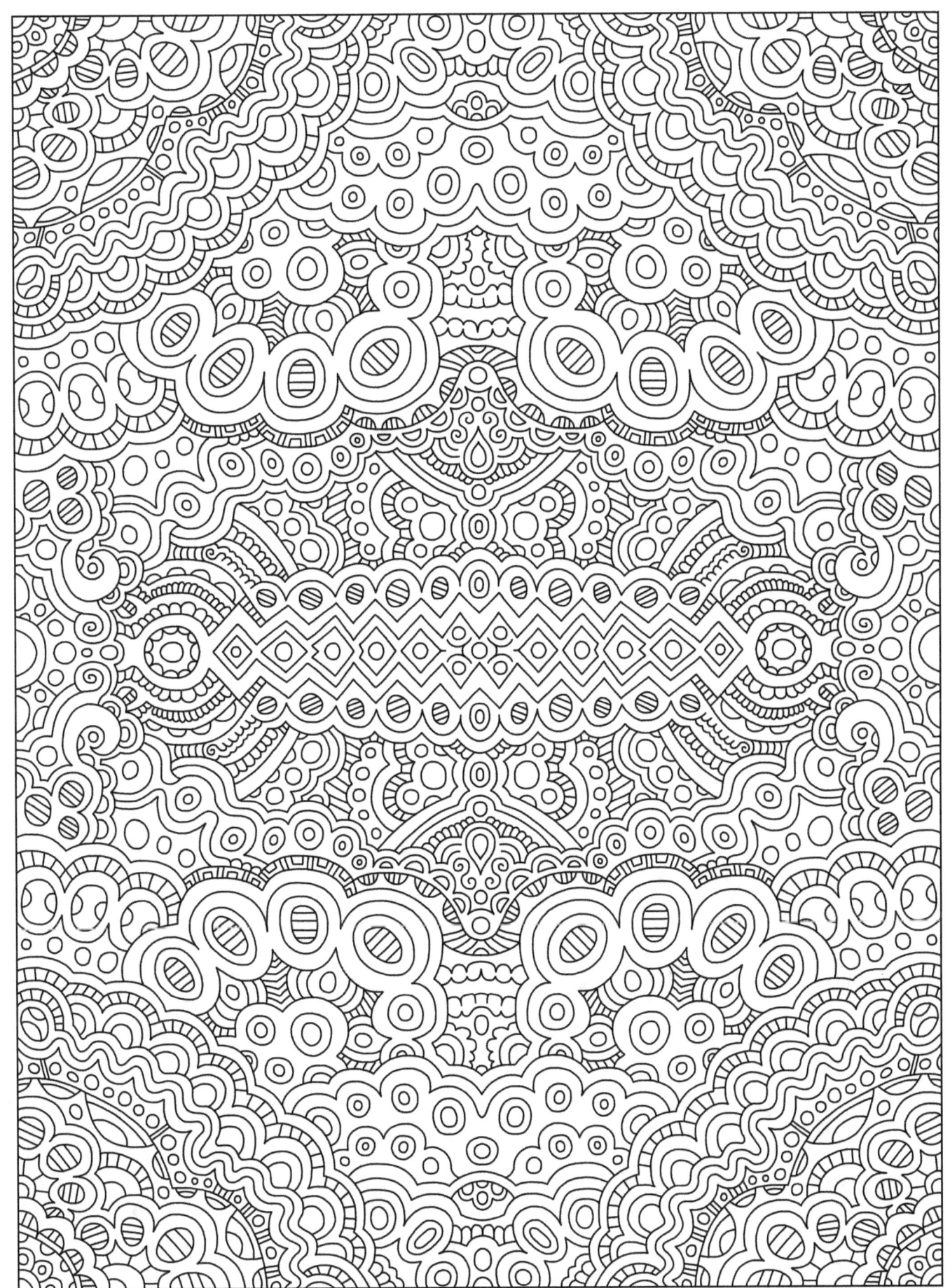

Drawing #19

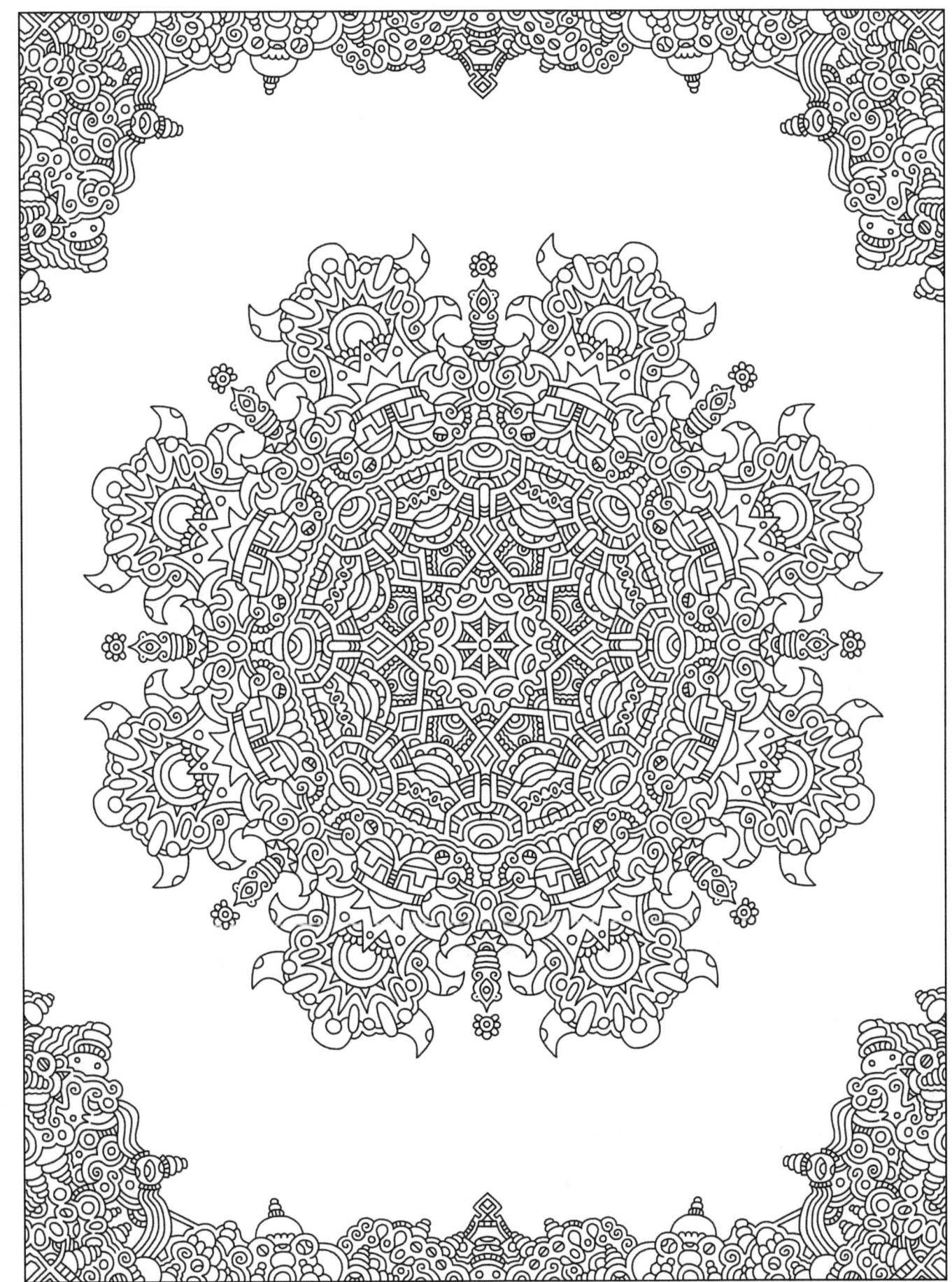

Drawing #20

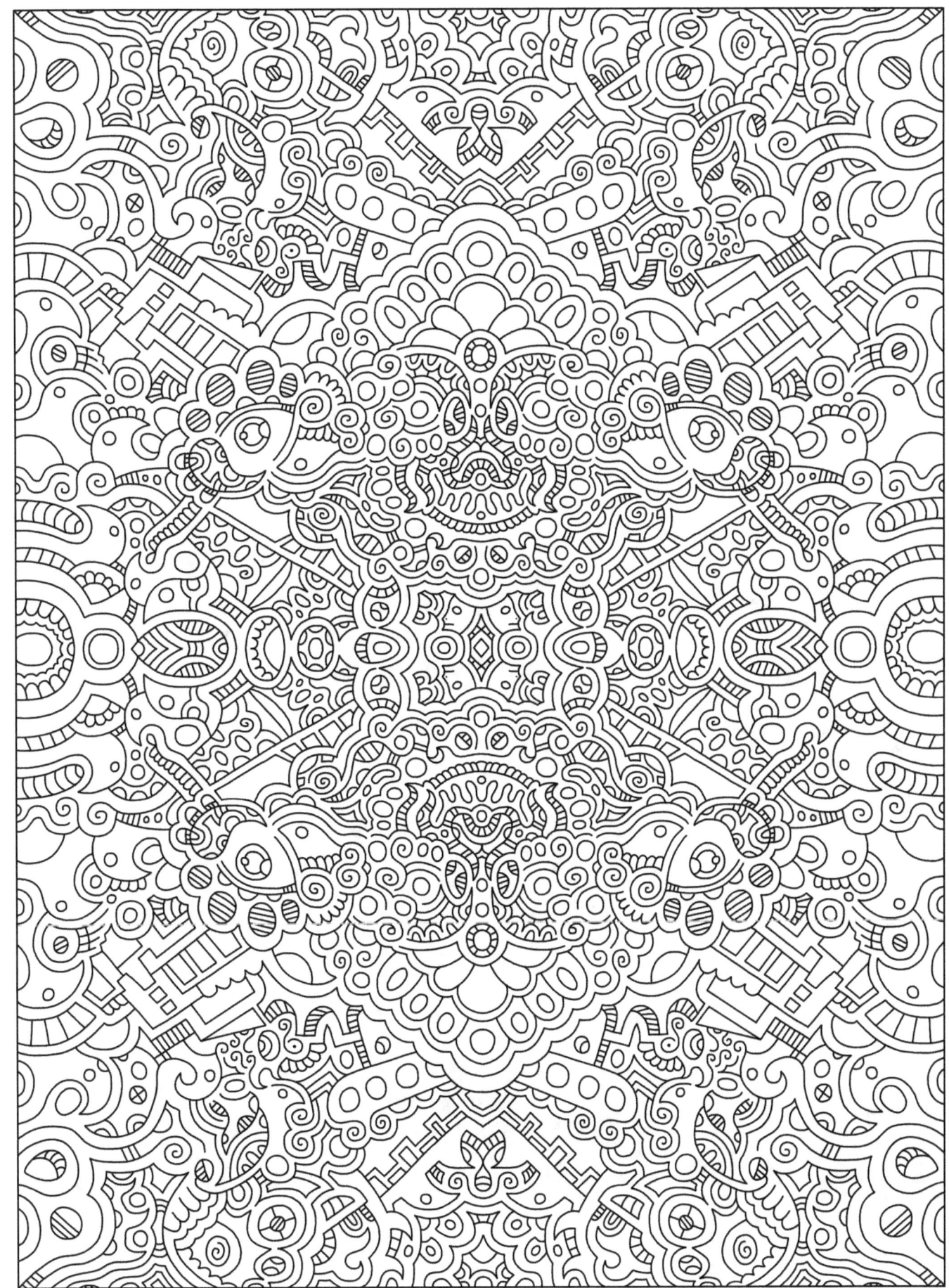

Drawing #21

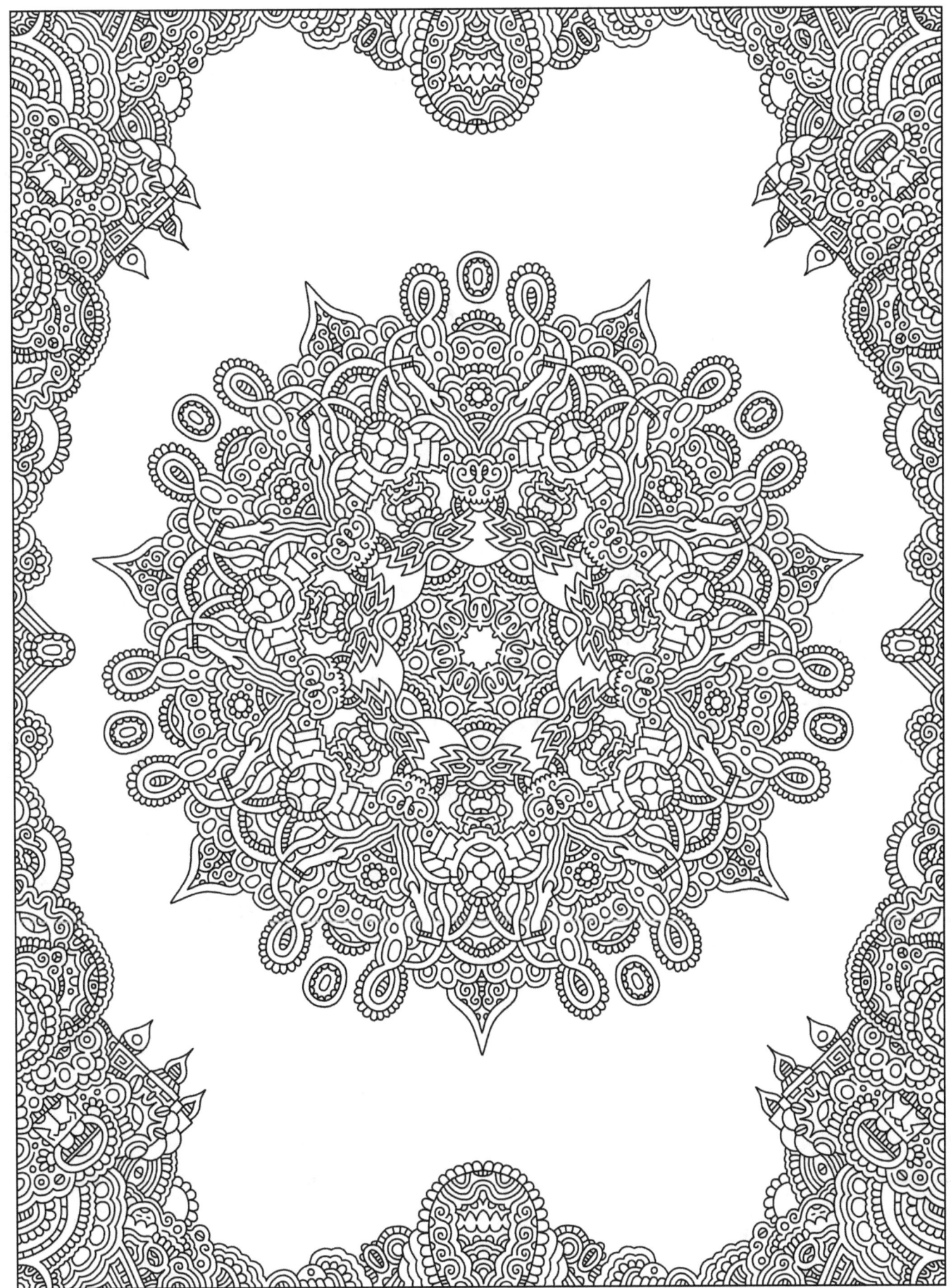

Drawing #22

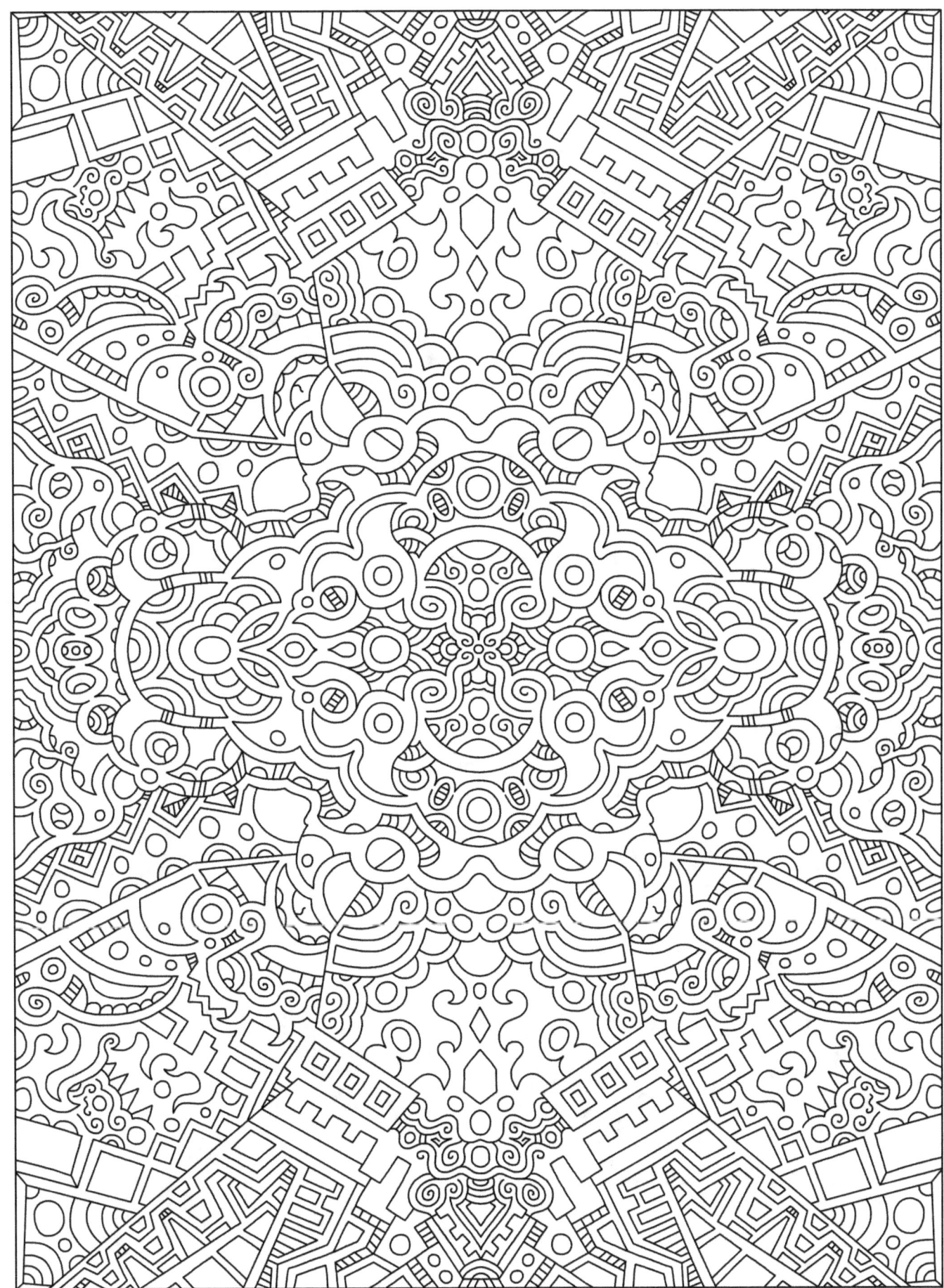

Drawing #23

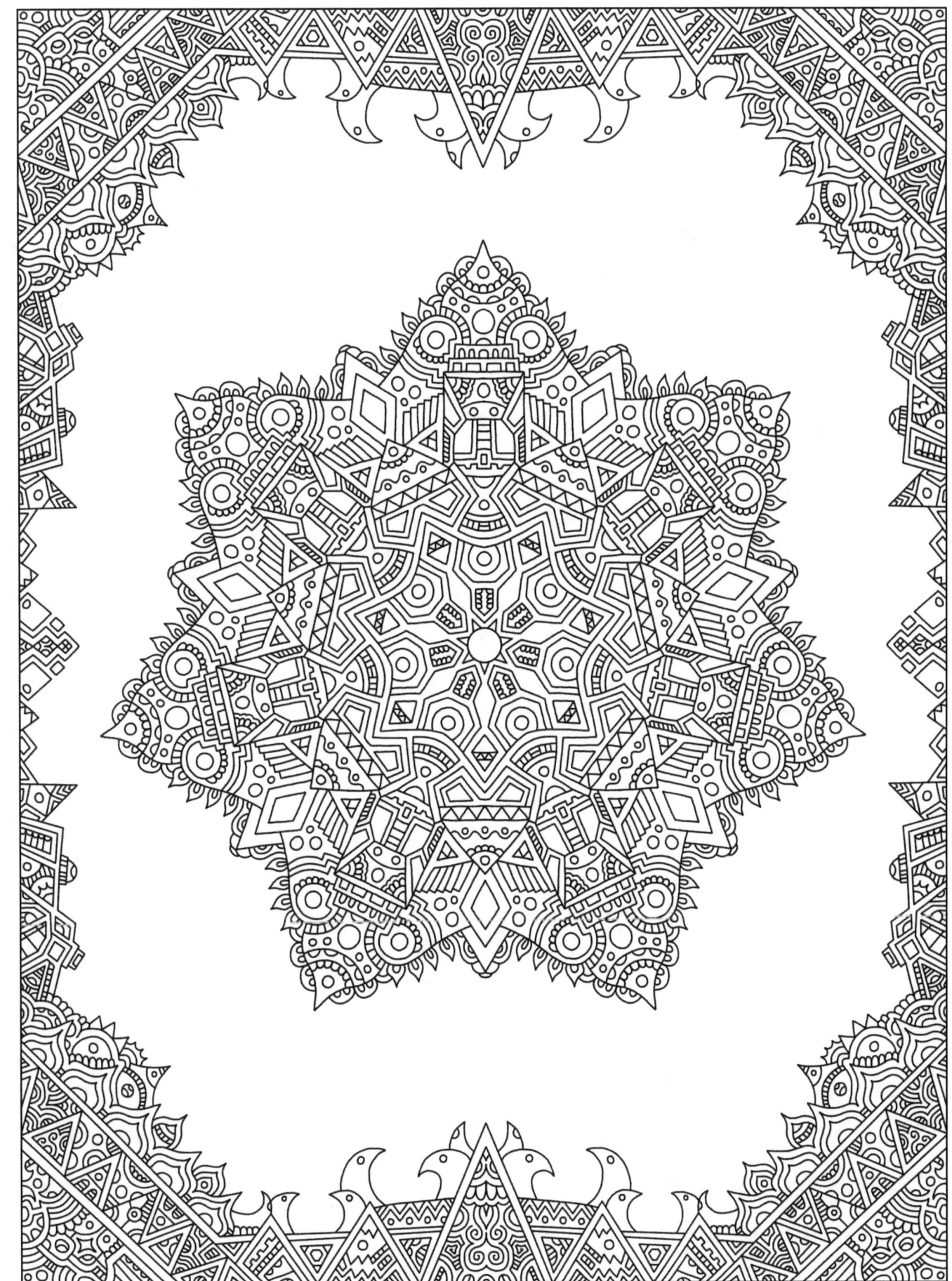

Drawing #24

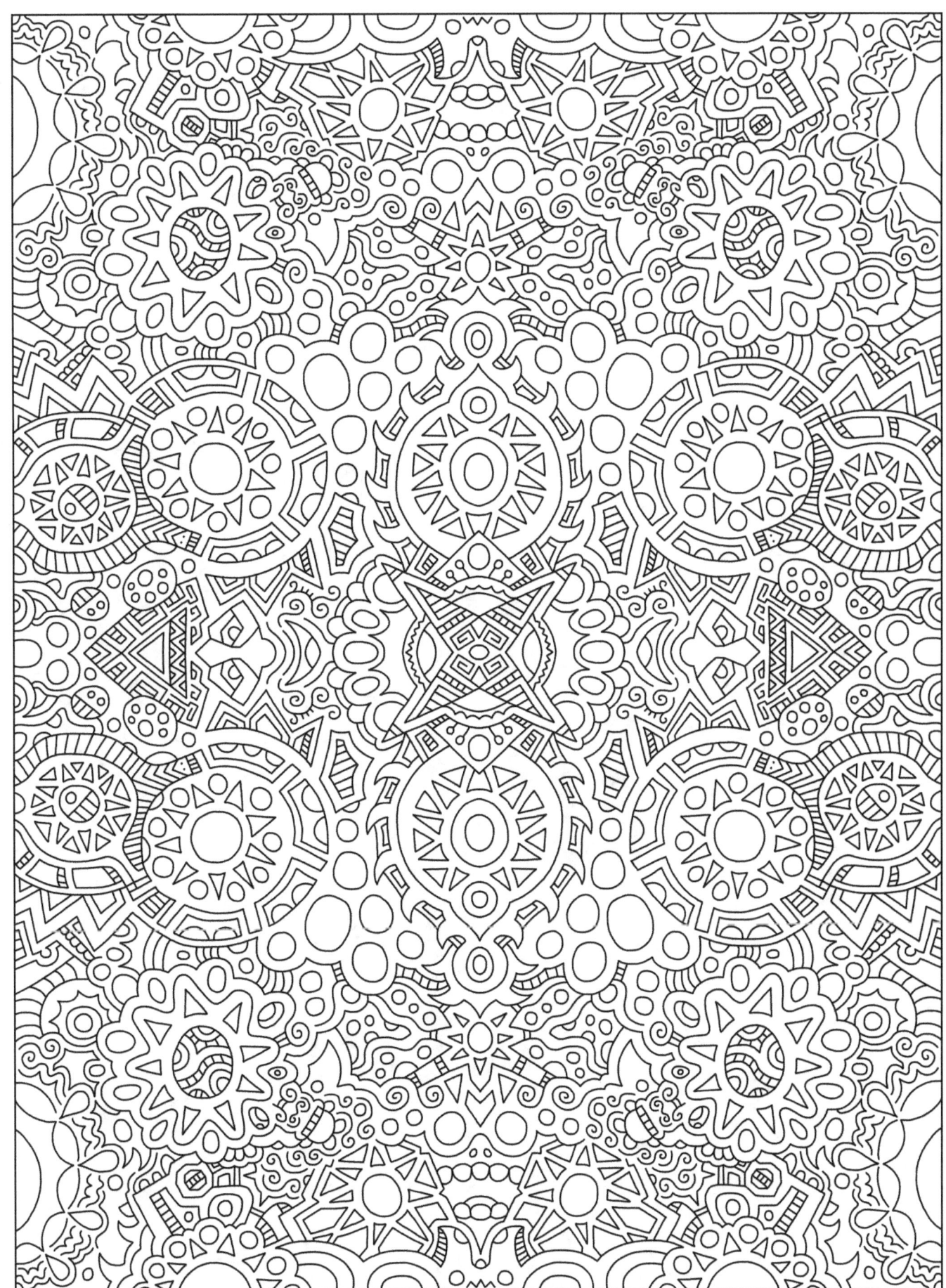

Drawing #25

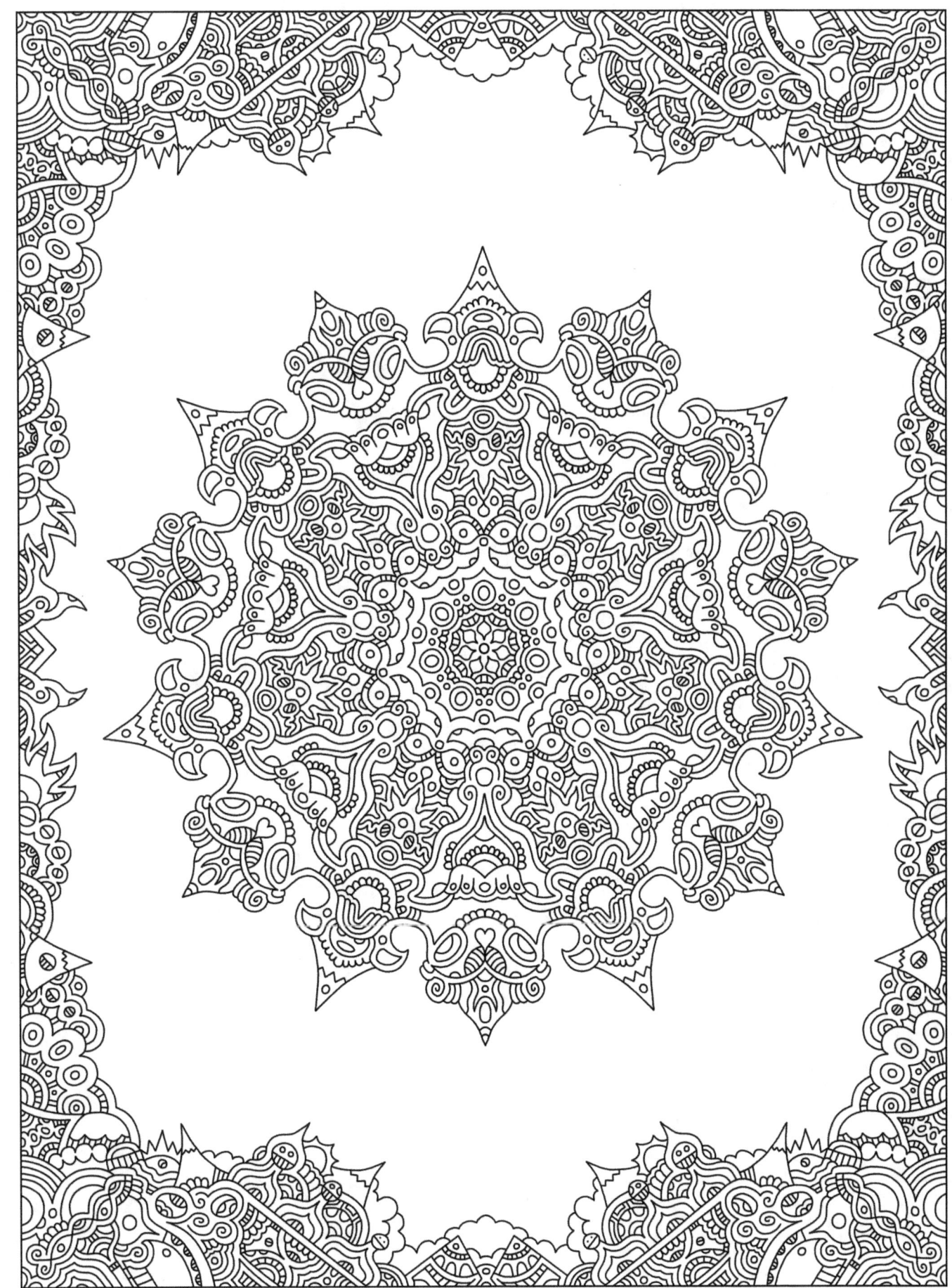

Drawing #26

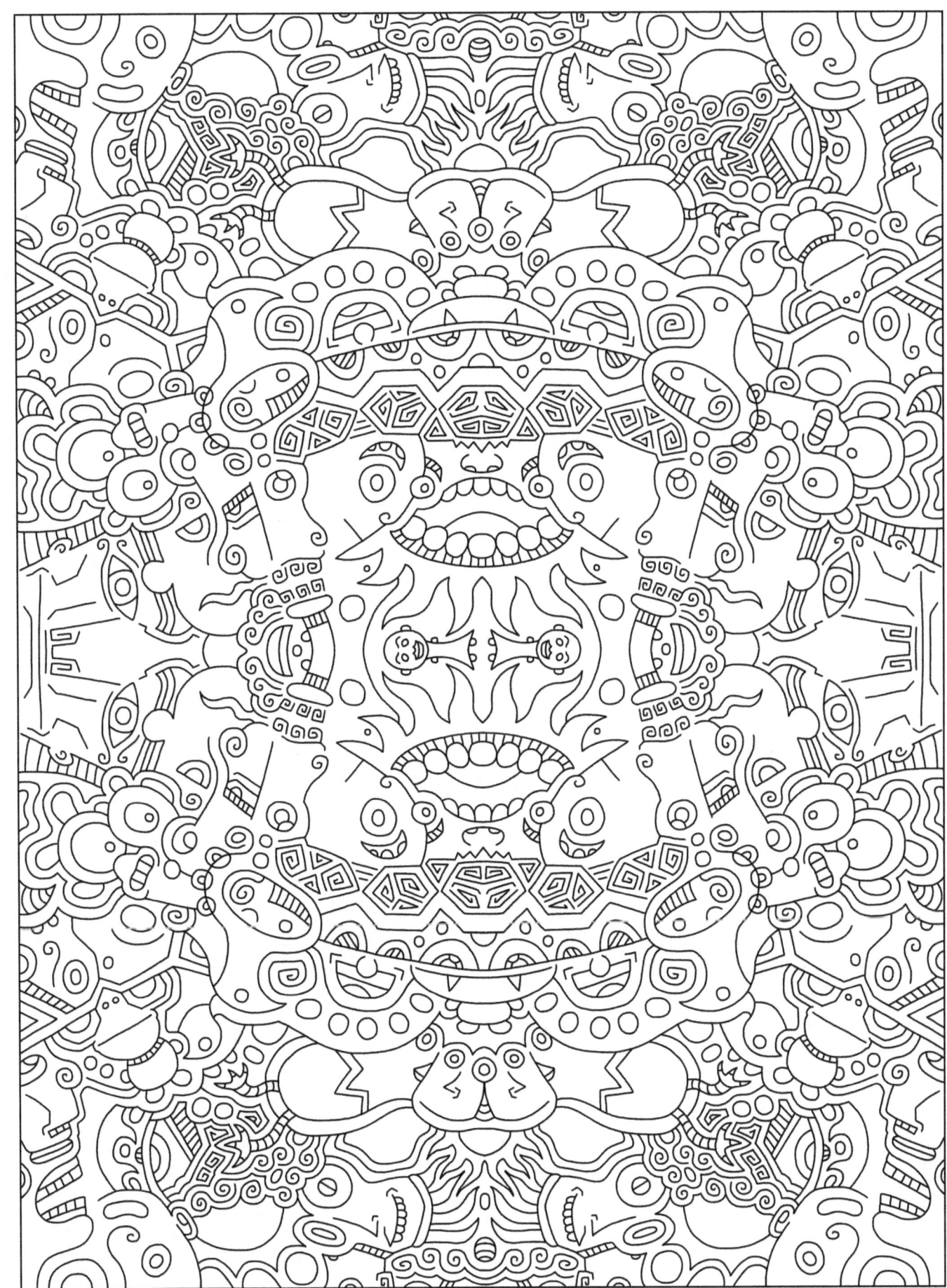

Drawing #27

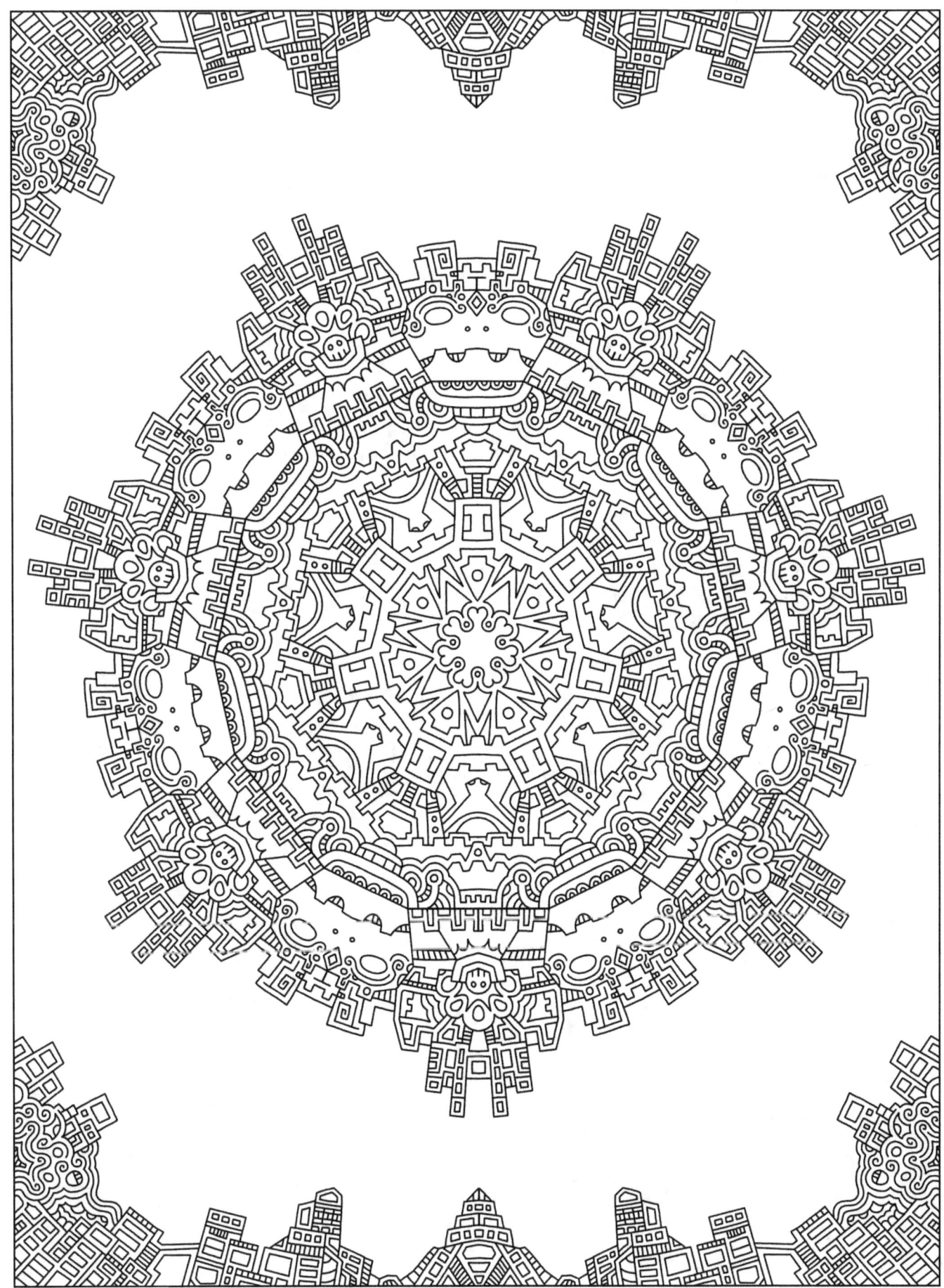

Drawing #28

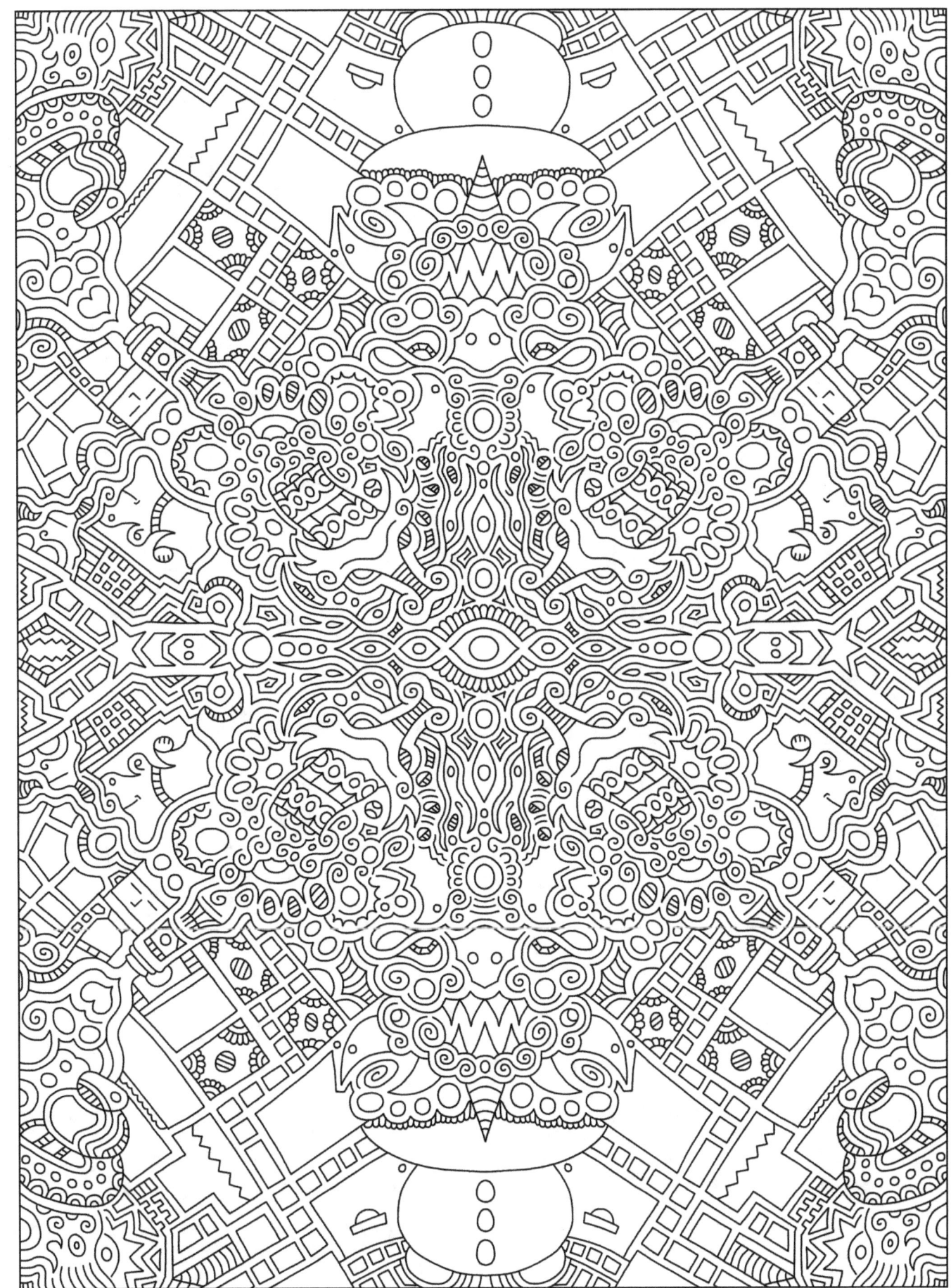

Drawing #29

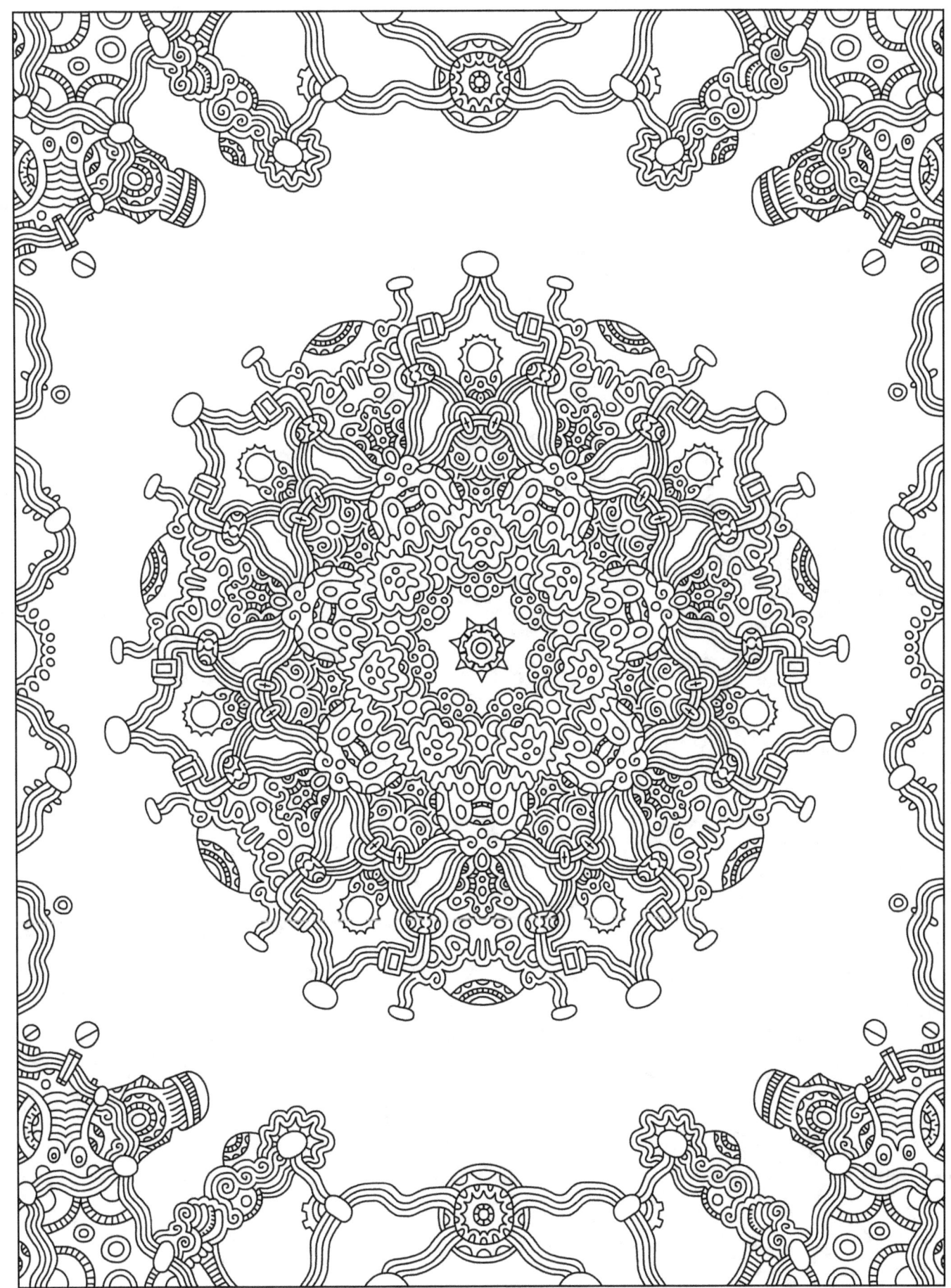

Drawing #30

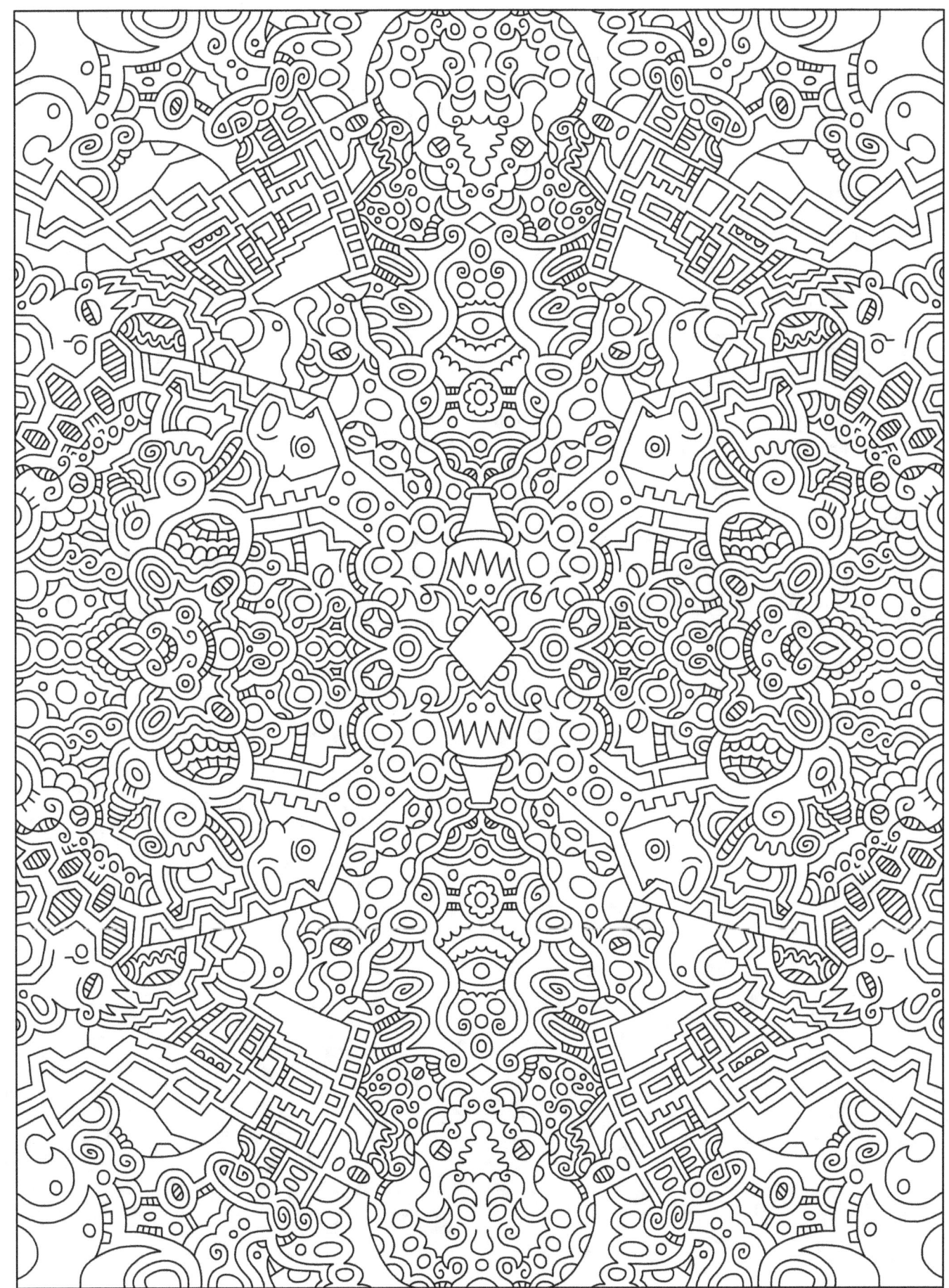

Drawing #31

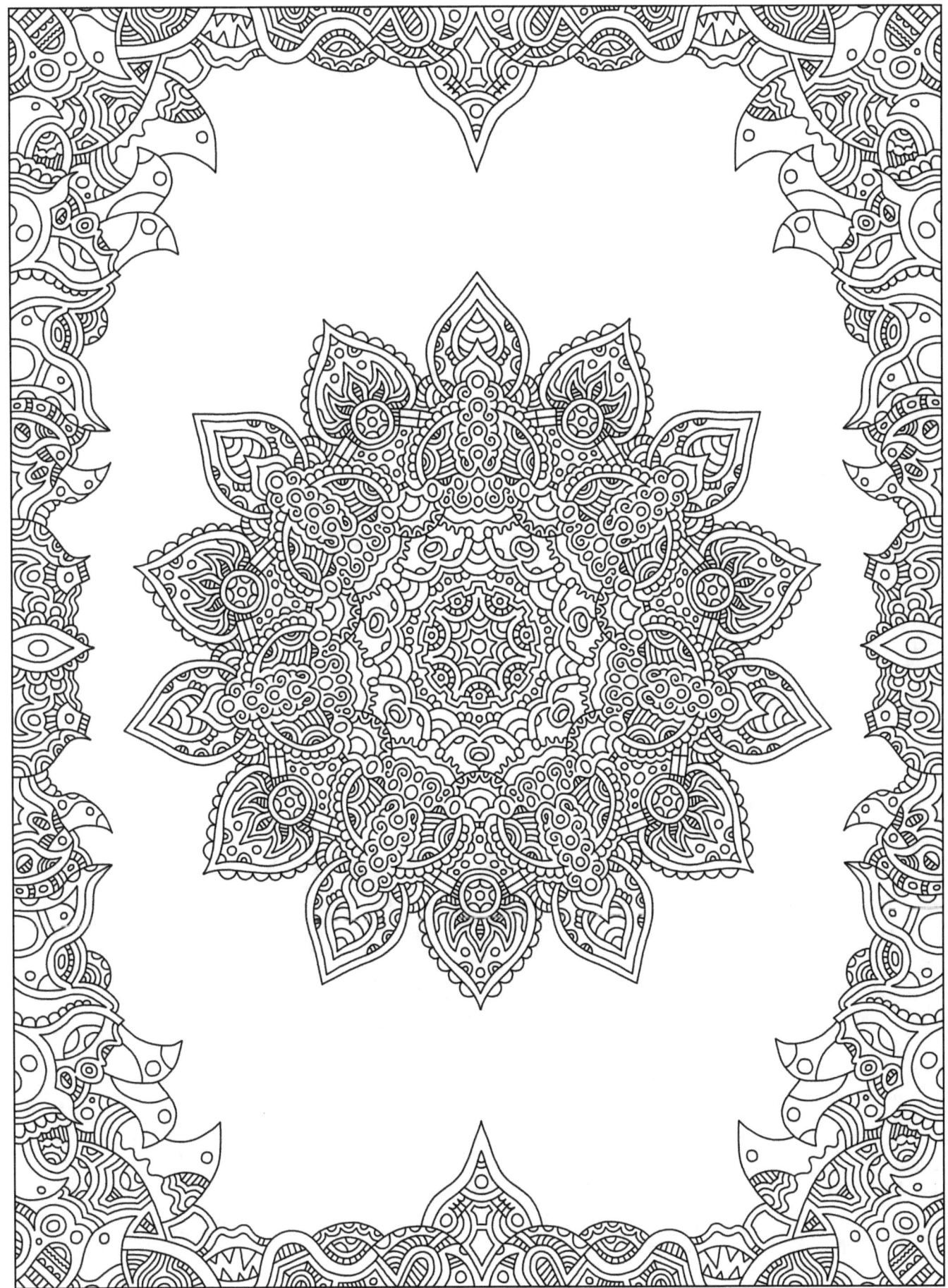

Drawing #32

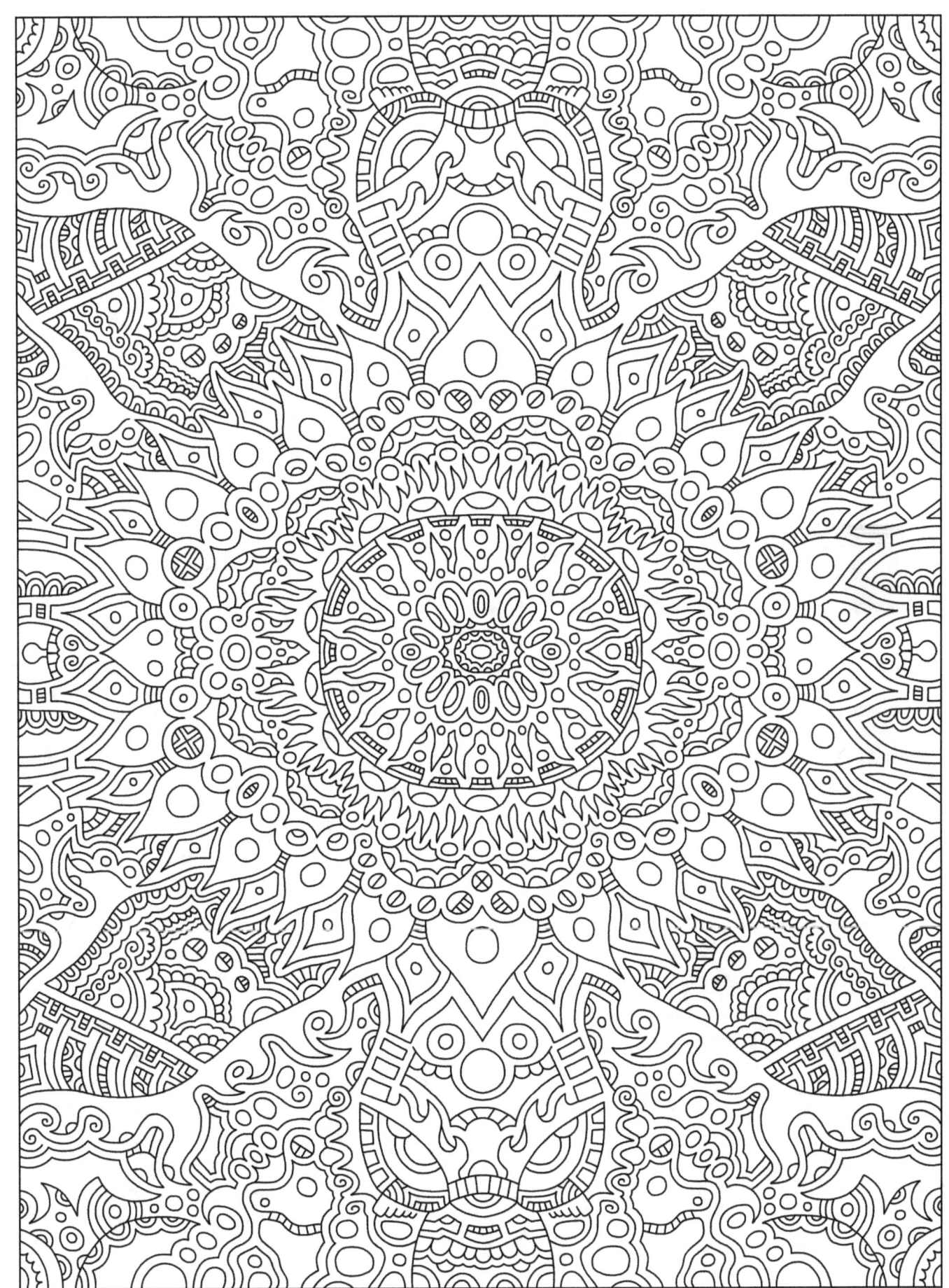

Drawing #33

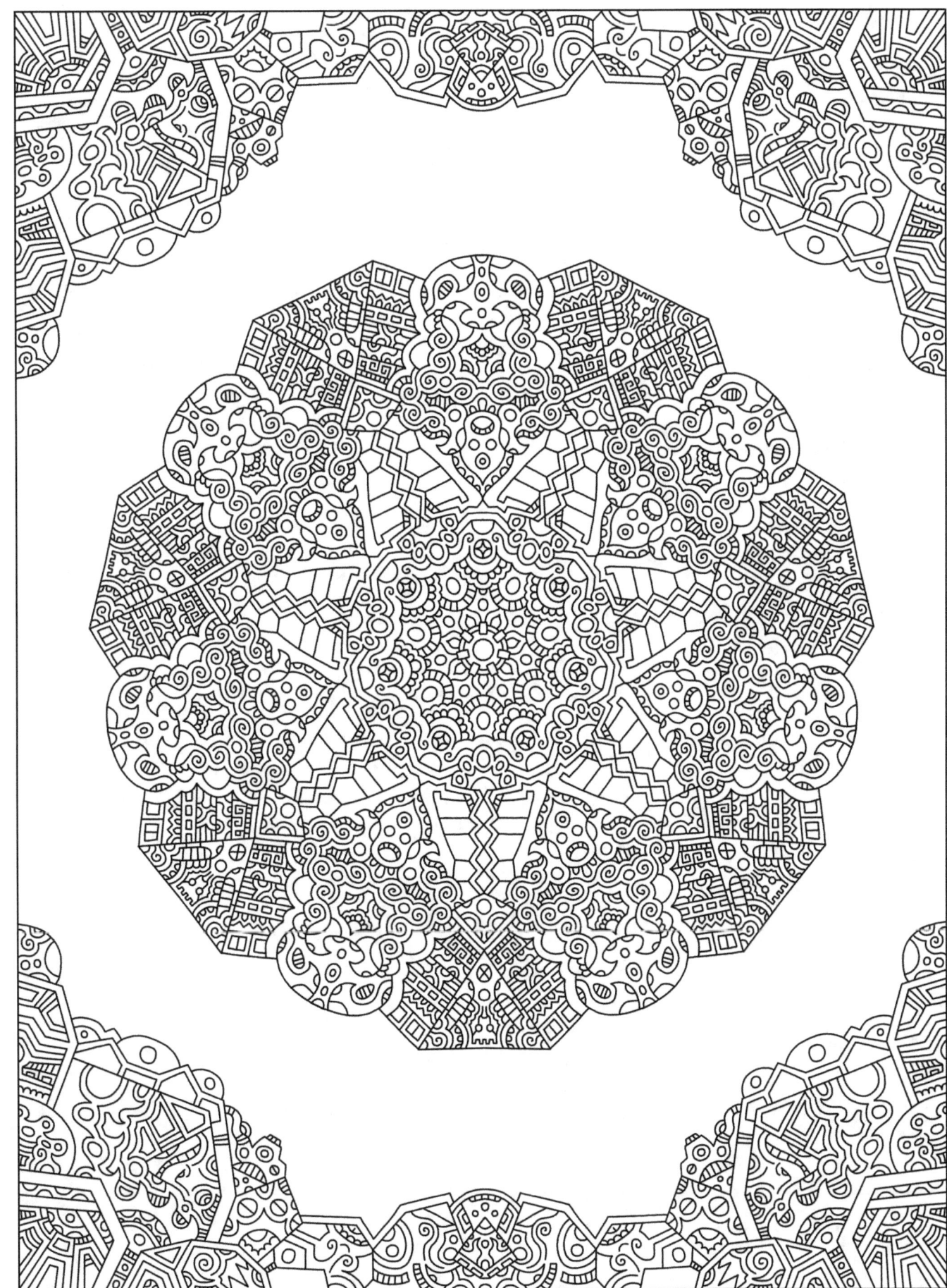

Drawing #34

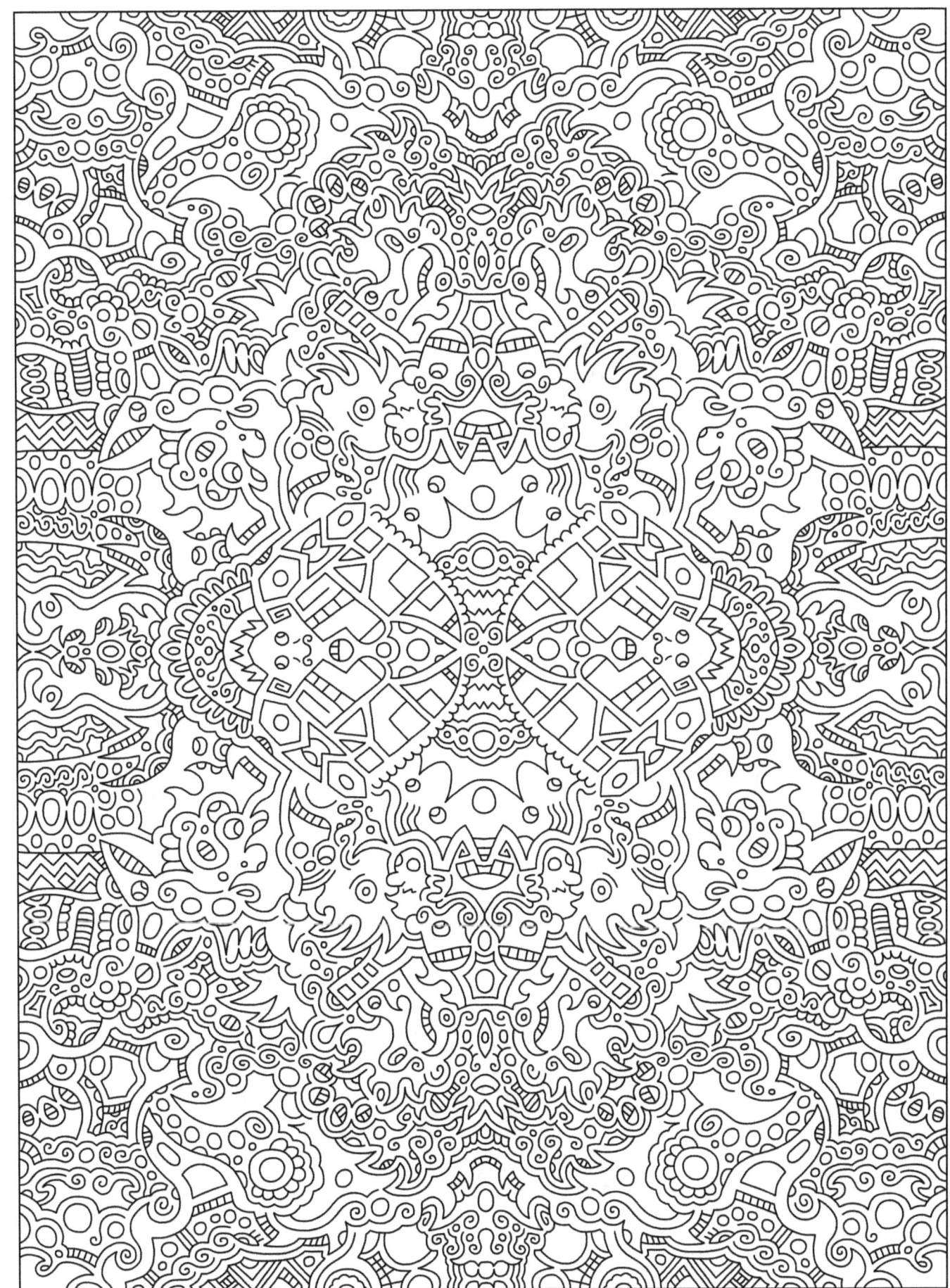

Drawing #35

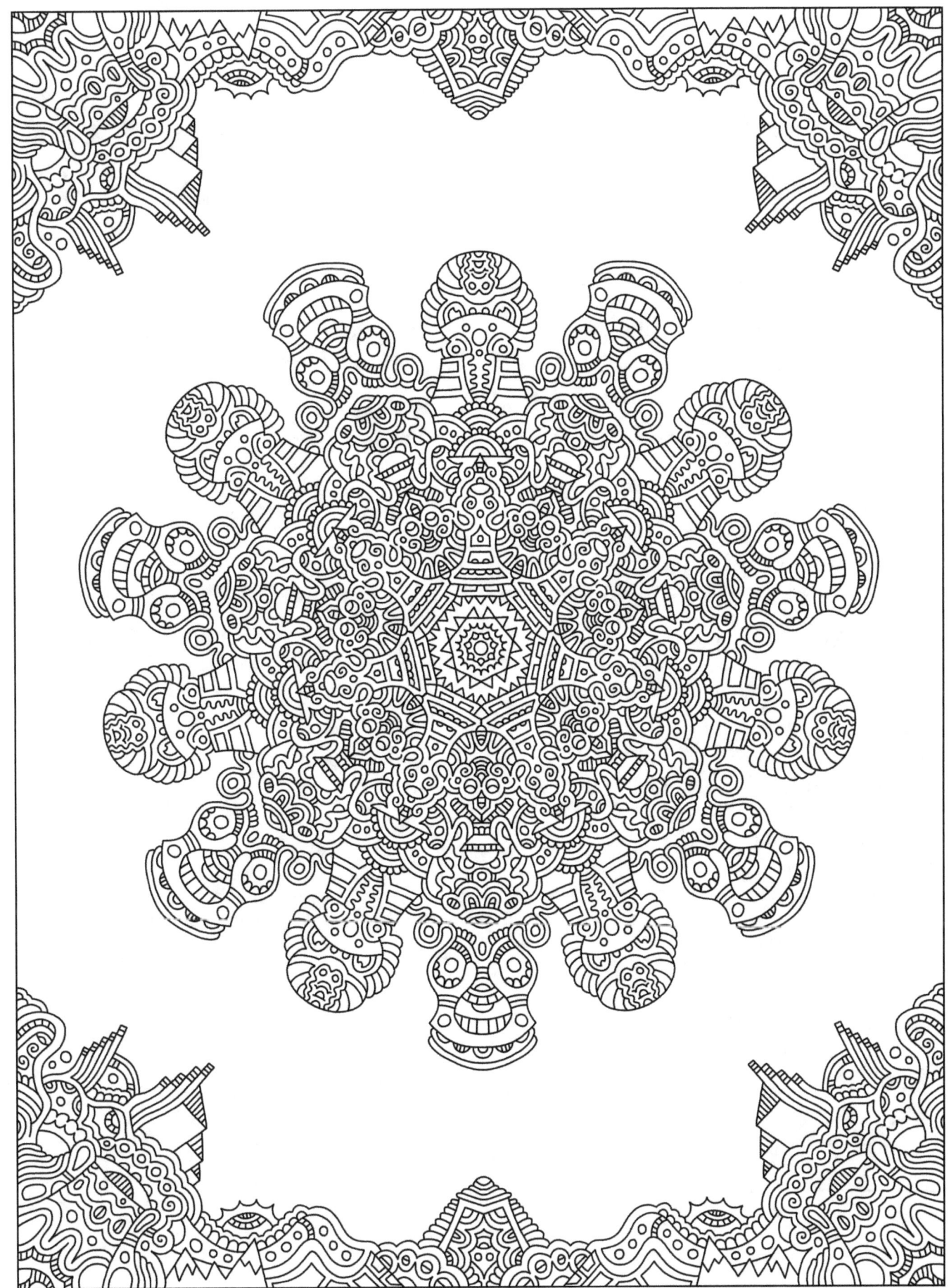

Drawing #36

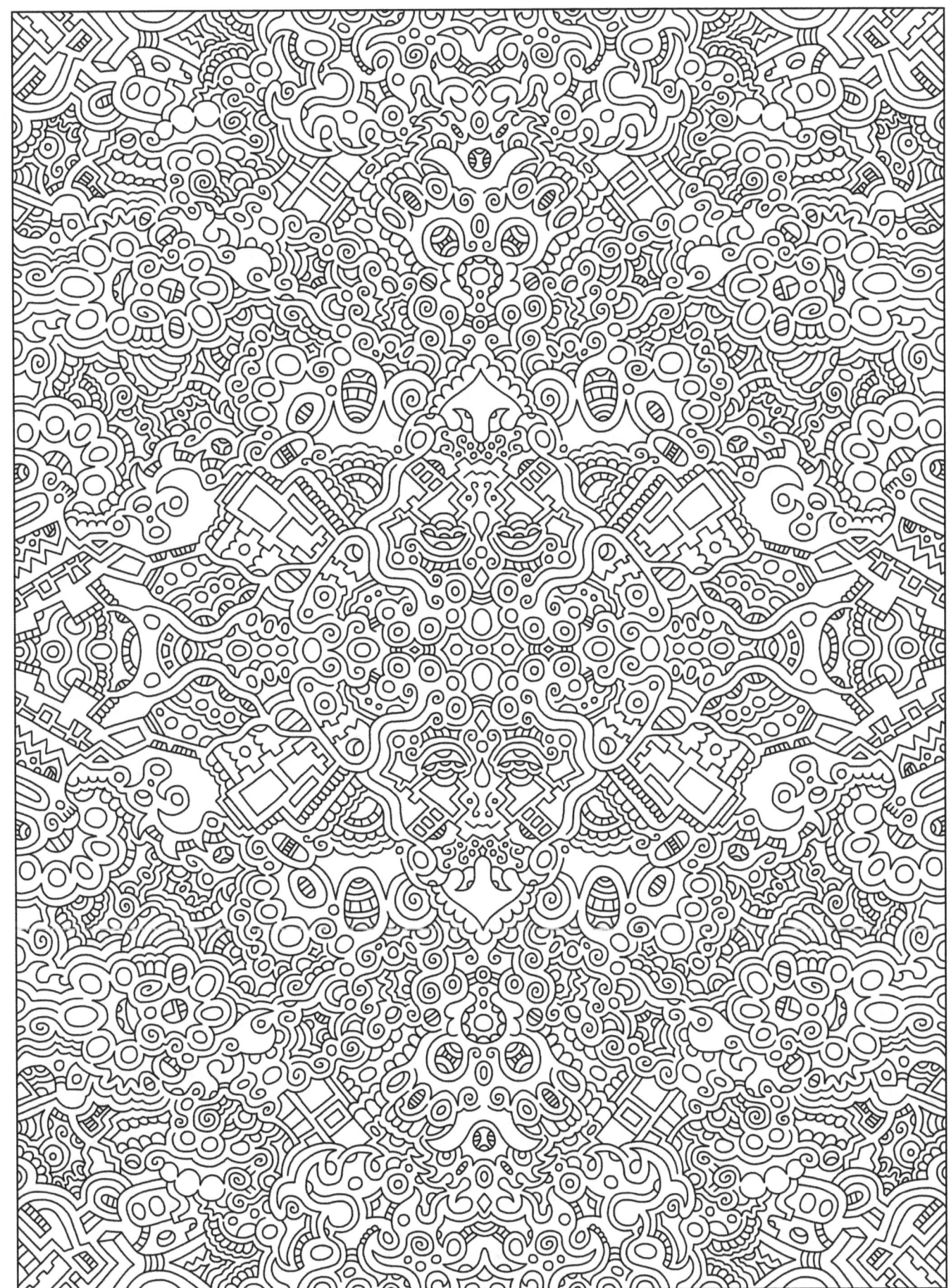

Drawing #37

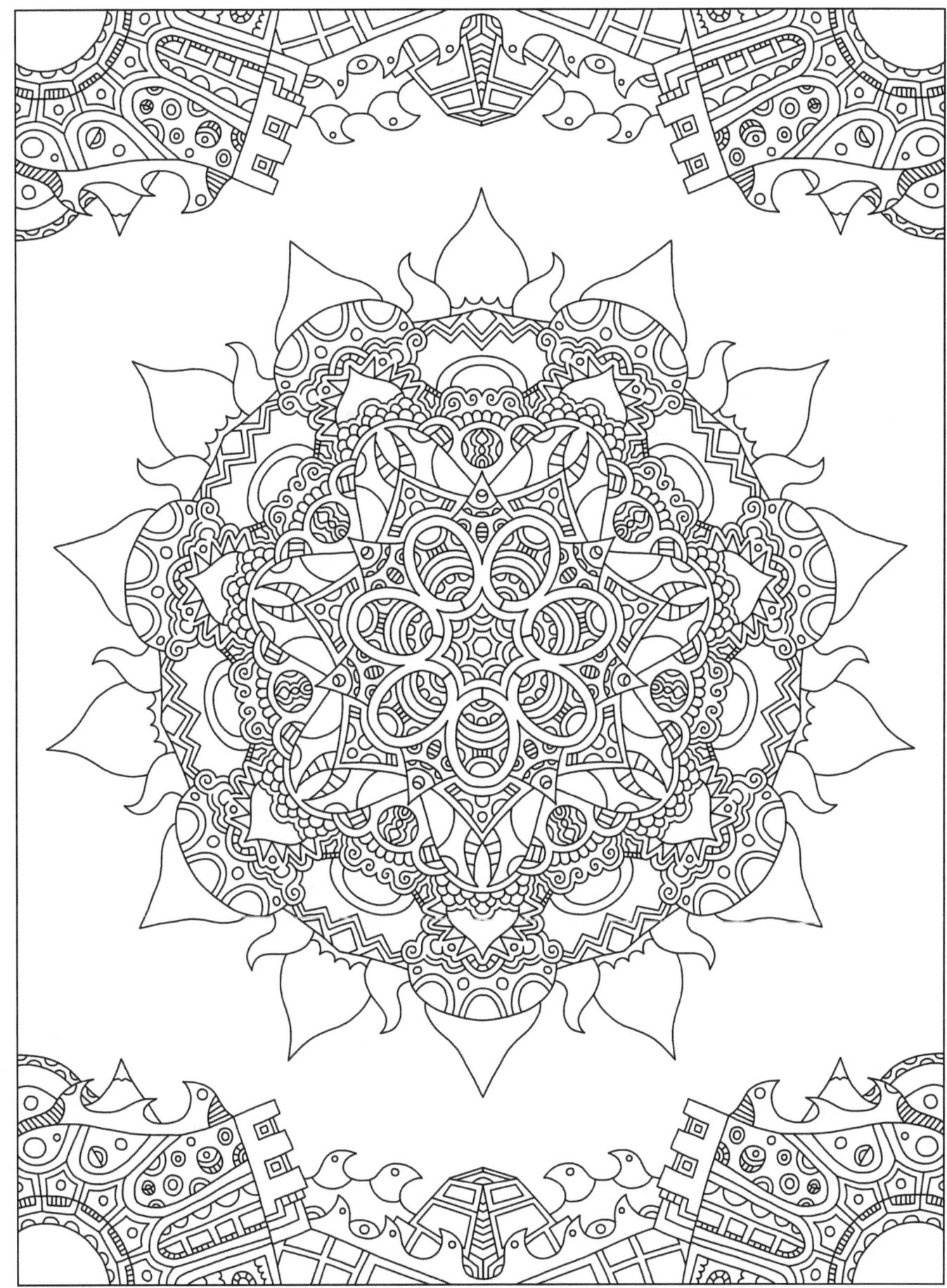

Drawing #38

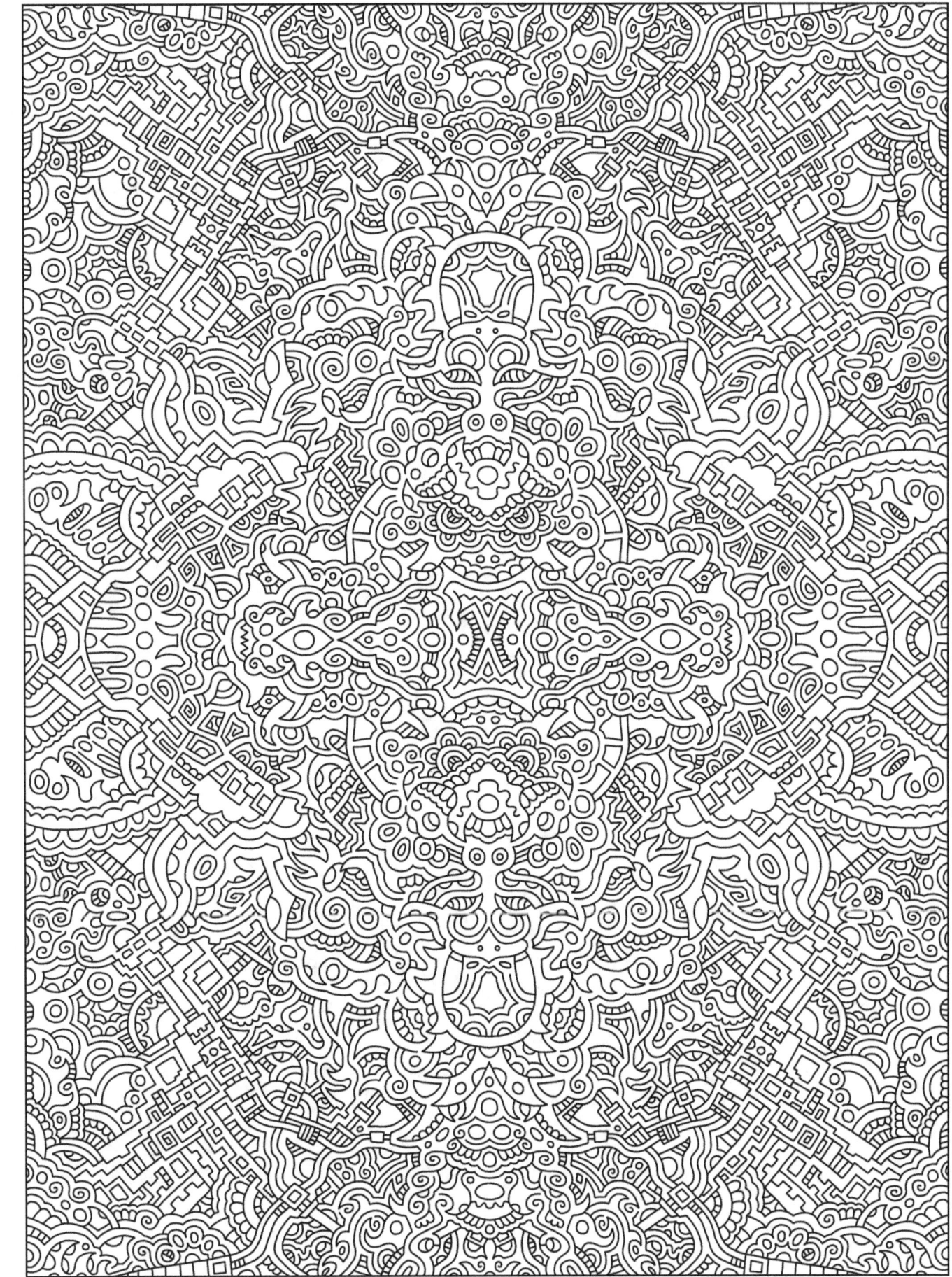

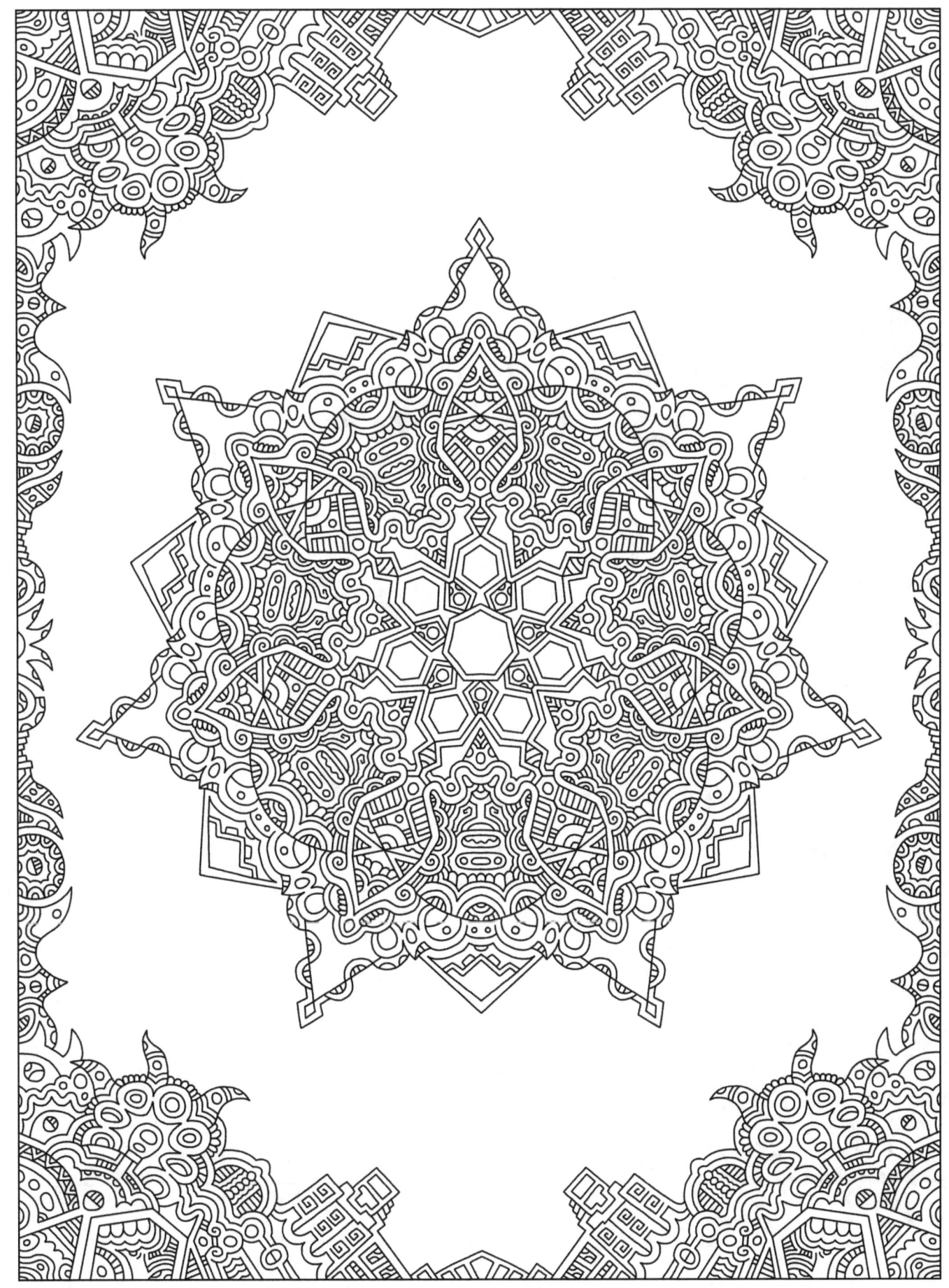

Drawing #40

www.ingramcontent.com/pod-product-compliance
Lightning Source LLC
Chambersburg PA
CBHW080517220526
45465CB00006B/2518